Dedication

This book is dedicated to all of those who helped me create this book; especially my angel helpers! I feel so blessed to have so many angels in my life.

Acknowledgements

Thank you to all the angels who are constantly supporting and guiding me; I couldn't have done this without you! My heart is filled with gratitude for all the gifts and experiences you have shared with me. I thank my family and friends for believing in me, especially when my angels guided me to challenge the status quo. I am so blessed to have so many loving people in my life who believe in me.

Special Thanks

A very special thank you to all those who helped make this book possible! You are truly angels here on earth and I appreciate you! Thank you to my editors and proof readers: Christine Webb, Jan Lund, and Anne Starke. Thank you also to all those who helped fund this book's production and to those who contributed real angel stories. Many blessings to you all!

Table of Contents

Introduction

A Note to the Reader

Dear reader, I am writing this book for you. I have had so many incredible experiences and life-altering shifts since I started working with angels. My hope is that you, too, can experience the magic angels can help bring to your life. We are taught to believe that life is staid, practical, and scientific, and indeed it can be viewed that way, but many of the things I have seen and experienced can be described as miracles.

I have organized this book in a way that made sense to me but please feel free to jump around. There is no right way to read this book. Since there may be terms that not everyone knows, I have included a helpful terms section towards the back of the book. I have defined these terms as I understand them, so please note that some people may have a different definition of some of these terms.

This book does share some of the same information as my first book "Life and the After Life: Notes from a Medium and Angel Communicator"; I feel some of the information is relevant in this book as well and I would not want to assume that everyone has read both of my books.

This book is about my beliefs and perspective and I encourage everyone to follow their own heart in terms of their beliefs. This is not an academic research book and should not be treated as such. There are academic books about angels out there, should you desire to read one. I have listed several resources at the back of the book that provide information on angels, spirituality, and related topics.

I hope that this book will help you connect with the spiritual aspect of life. I am also hopeful that you will better understand how to ask for and receive help from all the wonderful helpers we all have, and that you can begin to change your life in magical ways. Life truly is a wondrous journey and it feels that way when you connect with your angels and receive their help.

Happy Reading!

ONE

My Story

It is difficult to know where to begin this story. I will start at the beginning and as I remember it; the beginning happens to be before I was born. My first memory is of the other side. I feel that it is important to share this because I have always known that this physical life is not truly the beginning and it is not all there is. When I die, I know that I will carry on and this knowledge is such an inextricable part of who I am and how I view the world. Knowing that there was something before this life has helped me be open to some ideas that some others might have declared impossible. Having experienced the other side, the idea that angels are real beings was not such a far-fetched concept to me. Still, as I grew up, I fought hard to deny the fact that there is a spiritual side of life because I, like many of us in modern times, was raised to deny my spiritual self. As it sometimes happens, in order to see the light, I had to experience the darkness. What follows is an abbreviated version of my path to the light and the angels.

The Beginning

I cannot truly begin my story or tell you about angels without sharing the first memory I have from this life which happens to be just before I was born.

I am in a circle of beings that emanate light, no that isn't right, they seem to actually be made of light. It is beautiful as each being appears like moving light. When I say that I am in the circle, I mean that I am a part of the circle. There are seven of us including myself, and we seem to be standing there though we are not actually standing on anything; we are just there somehow. A conversation is taking place though it is not spoken out loud. We seem to instantly hear each other's thought or intent. I know that I need to leave this place and I am sad to leave. The others are encouraging me, telling me what I already know, that I need to go now and that I have a lot I need to do where I am going. I am so reluctant. It isn't so much that the place I am going is bad; it is just that I love the place where I am. And then I leave and I am no longer in this place.

So that is my first memory. It is simple and short; I don't know why I remember that particular moment but not what happened before. I don't remember exactly what happened next either but I do know that I have very early memories from this life. Perhaps I was meant to remember the other side maybe that was all part of the plan.

There are many people who will probably chalk up this memory to my time in the womb. I can tell you that I feel in my heart this was not simply a memory of the womb, though the body I would join was likely in the womb when I experienced this memory. I cannot explain the circle of light beings as a womb experience. I am not trying to convince anyone because I feel that everyone needs to decide what they believe. I am just sharing my memories and beliefs with you.

Growing up, I was a sensitive child, though I would not have realized this if you'd asked. It often happens that we do not realize something about a moment until much, much later. I did however always feel different from others, a sense that heightened as I got older and became particularly strong in high school. I remember looking around and thinking to myself that I was not coming from the same place as my peers. I don't think this is a unique experience by any means, but nevertheless, I didn't feel like an everyday teenager.

It is true that I was different from many others I grew up with – I was born abroad and English was not my first language. Though I don't have an accent, when I first came to the United States, I was, for all intents and purposes, a foreigner. I didn't speak English, I was used to different food, and I moved from a rural French village to urban California – it was a huge shock! Even with these differences, I sensed that what I felt was something deeper.

Though I didn't talk about it growing up, I saw and sensed ghosts and spirits. Sometimes I saw them with my physical eyes, but more often than not I saw them with my third eye. The third eye is our energetic eye and is now believed to be centered in the middle of our brains in the pineal gland. I didn't understand that then though, I just knew that when I closed my eyes I "saw" a lot in my mind. Sometimes these images were beautiful moving pictures like something you'd see in a kaleidoscope and sometimes the images were dark. I know now that the darker images were often connected with the ghosts and spirits. It was like I was seeing their mental state. Sometimes I think they were even showing me these images on purpose. I didn't really understand all of this at the time though.

As a result of being more aware and open to spirits and energy beings, I initially had some traumatic experiences with angry ghosts and entities who created and then fed on the energy of fear. I didn't know who to turn to or who to tell. I didn't think my parents could help because I was pretty sure that they didn't experience this for themselves. I also didn't think talking about it at school was a good idea and I had a fear of being labeled as crazy (I have sometimes wondered if I was burned as a witch in a past life). In all seriousness, many seers have been persecuted in other times so this was a legitimate fear in some ways.

I won't go into detail about the experiences I had with ghosts, but I could certainly say that I felt haunted by them. It was frightening, particularly as an adolescent when I was shown very dark things. Sometimes these angry spirits would even break things in my home or affect my appliances so that the TV would turn itself on and play a horror movie. The most intense experiences occurred when a spirit tried to enter my body. This was very much like it was depicted in the movie *Ghost,* though Patrick Swayze was a nice ghost and some of the ghosts that were around me did not seem so nice. I needed to learn boundaries and how to manage my gifts, but in order to do that; I needed to talk about what was happening.

Because I feared being judged, and the fear was so crippling, I didn't talk about my experiences until I was an adult. I had to go through my own journey and I tried for years and years to ignore my gifts. I finally ended up shutting down completely rather than acknowledging what I saw and felt. You can read more about this journey in my first book, "Life and the After-Life." As a result of shutting down, I ended up in my early thirties in a very dark place. I was emotionally struggling, unemployed, in a bad marriage and physically ill. Every aspect of my life was in crisis! I went to a clairvoyant reader, desperate for guidance, and she helped me to see that when I shut down, I closed myself off to information that I needed as well. This resonated for me and I started the process of opening back up and investigating this realm I had previously shut out. What I learned was positive and affirming. I started to read voraciously and I took classes from local and well-known teachers that specialized in clairvoyance, energy work, and working with ghosts, spirits, and angels.

It was shortly after my appointment with the clairvoyant reader that I had a profound experience that would forever alter how I viewed reality. I was in Seattle and had just learned that my marriage was falling apart; I was unemployed and felt utterly lost. Everything I'd thought was stable in my life was in upheaval. I prayed for help; I didn't know what I needed, I just knew I needed something because I felt lost. During this time, I was suffering from insomnia and was on sleeping pills. One afternoon after a nearly sleepless night, I decided to take a nap. After about an hour, I woke to some very loud sounds. It wasn't just loud; I was vibrating with the noise. What was more incredible was what I felt! I experienced the most incredible outpouring of love in those moments. The sensation is hard to describe, but I felt surrounded by incredible, overwhelming love that seemed to envelop me in the most comforting way. The sound was loud and unmistakable – it was the sound of angel wings beating. There were so many that I couldn't even begin to imagine how many wings it would take to create that much noise! The sounds of so many wings led me to believe there were many angels with me at that moment. The experience was so incredible that I cried with joy. This lasted for a period of time, and I have no idea how long it lasted, but time seemed to stretch in those moments.

When it ended and I lay in bed, I knew that my perspective was forever altered. I also knew that whatever happened, I would be okay. In the months that followed, there were many times I thought back to that moment and was comforted by the memory of the experience. They had confirmed that I was not alone and that I had their loving support.

After I had this experience, I wondered why I had not had angelic experiences earlier and why the spirit experiences I'd had were of the darker variety. Then I learned something profound. I learned that we all have free will in this life, and part of that free will involves the ability to choose to do things on our own or to ask for help. I equate our minds, lives, and energy fields to a garden. If you don't plant flowers, weeds automatically show up. You don't need to plant them or even water them for them to thrive. Angry ghosts and spirits are like weeds – they don't need an invitation into your life. Angels on the other hand are like flowers – you need to "plant" them or invite them in order to have them in your garden or life. You also have to "water" them or continually ask for their help. I had never experienced angels because I had never asked for help! I had simply struggled on my own. This was not my fault, because I didn't know to ask for their help. I would like everyone to know that help is available - all you have to do is ask.

After my experience of hearing angel wings, my life changed dramatically. I left my husband, relocated back to Colorado, and decided to get certified to teach English as a second language outside of the country since the economy was so bad in the United States. I chose to get my teaching certification in Spain and it was a truly magical experience!

Barcelona proved to be just the place I needed to heal my wounded heart. It was a place where people were friendly, the culture was fun, and they *loved* the nightlife. I was in love! Here were my people! Dinner was eaten from 9 pm to midnight and *then* people went out. It was incredible! I let myself be whimsical and I loved this new, less practical me. Life was a lot more fun! I had class during the day which involved observing and also teaching, but my nights were free and I took full advantage of the night culture.

My time there was filled with going out and having Clara (a lovely drink made with what they call lemonade and beer), eating tapas in the street cafés, and going to nightclubs and street festivals. It was a dreamlike, incredible experience; such a heavenly contrast to the last couple of months that I could scarcely believe how amazing it felt to be alive. A lot of the weight I'd been holding onto just melted off; it was like I was shedding my old self.

I loved the street festivals and got in the habit of going nearly every night of the week. This was totally impractical because they went late into the night and I still had to get up at 7 a.m. or so, but it didn't matter. I think I'd been so starved for fun in the last several years that I couldn't seem to get enough of it!

I can recall one particular week when I'd been out three nights in a row until 2:30 or 3:00 a.m. and I went out the next night anyway. That is the culture in Spain, so when I started to say goodnight to my new friends at 1:30 a.m., everyone was surprised because it was *so* early (by Spanish standards anyway) to be going home. I said my goodbyes and started to walk home since I had to teach the next morning at 8:30 am. I walked back in the direction I remembered coming from but it was dark and I had not walked home by myself from there before. The farther I walked the thinner the crowd became until eventually I was alone. I had been walking for about twenty minutes when I came to realize that I didn't know where I was and nothing looked familiar. I wasn't panicky but I was certainly concerned. I was lost, feeling the effect of the liquor, and in a foreign country where I didn't speak the language in the middle of the night. Panic could have set in but I didn't feel scared. I did however ask for the angels to help me. I felt a little silly speaking out loud so I just asked them silently in my mind.

After walking a few more blocks, I saw a woman ahead, sitting on a bench. She was by herself and the bench was not at a bus stop or anything and she didn't seem to be doing anything which was pretty odd at 2 a.m., even in Spain. She looked nice enough, so I approached her and said the name of the intersection where I was staying and gestured around to see if she could point me in the right direction. She stood up and started walking. Puzzled at first, I followed her, thinking that she must be leading me there. I tried to make conversation with her in the little Spanish that I knew so I introduced myself and asked what her name was and she responded, "Estelle." Since I knew very little Spanish and she apparently didn't speak English, we walked silently for several more blocks before we came to my flat. She walked me all the way to the door and then I thanked her profusely before going inside and collapsing with relief and exhaustion onto the bed.

As I was drifting to sleep, I thought about how odd it had been to run across that woman on the bench and how helpful she had been, and how she had walked me all the way home and wanted nothing in return. Then something dawned on me. She had walked me all the way to my door and I had only told her my intersection. And her name in Spanish means "star". And I had come upon her just after asking the angels for help. I suddenly had a totally different understanding of what might have happened. I cannot be sure but I do feel like I was helped by an angel that night. Whether the angels guided her to me, or whether she was an angel, I will never know. Either way, I am thankful for the help I received that night. Now I always ask for help from angels when I am in need.

Both of the experiences in Seattle and Barcelona helped me to believe that angels were real and could help me. These experiences helped me to trust in the divine that showed me that I was not on my own. Because these were such incredible experiences, I shared them with people I was close to. I was awestruck by what was happening and I needed to share this with others. Luckily we live in a time in which people are much more open. When I did open up and share, I was not judged as I had feared - in fact people were very supportive and often curious about what I experienced. Though it took me nearly 30 years to come to terms with what I sensed, when I did, I stopped viewing it as a sort of curse and embraced my experiences as a gift.

During the process of the exploration of my gifts, I learned that others could benefit when I "tuned in" to what I saw, heard, and felt from the spiritual realm. This was a revelation! I started doing readings first for friends, and then for paying clients. I don't believe anyone aspires to be a medium, clairvoyant, or ghost whisperer when they grow up and I did fight it at first, but gradually I came to realize that this was a part of my path. I honed my skills communicating with ghosts and learned how to help them cross over into the light. I also learned how to communicate with spirit guides and angels and how to protect myself from unwanted energy from ghosts and other people.

As I opened up even more and gave readings, I learned a great deal about ghosts, spirits, angels, and the after-life. In my first book, I shared some basic information about these topics but I feel compelled to share more about angels. I decided to share with readers some of the amazing things I have learned about angels and how they can help us in our lives.

The information I share in this book is a combination of information I have learned through my work with angels through clients, through my own life experiences, and from books and other materials about angels. My hope is that this book will help as a starting point for learning and open the door for their divine assistance in your life.

TWO

What is an angel?

Angels are energy beings who are here to help us with our missions and with everyday life. When translated, angel means "messenger" in Greek, and indeed it is believed that angels are the messengers who take our prayers to and from the creator and heaven. Angels are not specific to any religion and they are there for people of all faiths. Angels or angelic beings are described in Christianity, Judaism, Islam, and in many other faiths and cultures throughout the world.

Angels are one of my favorite topics to talk and write about and I could probably fill up 5 books with information about them! For me, angels have played a very important role in my life, but that is not the only reason why I love talking about them. I love them because once I started working with them and asking for their help, my life literally felt magical! I cannot stress this enough, when you honestly and openly ask for their assistance, problems are sometimes resolved so easily that you will pinch yourself and ask if you are dreaming. This is not always the case because sometimes angels help us answer our own prayers by helping us make changes and sometimes these take time. I have had prayers that were answered with amazing speed and others that required more faith and patience. I will discuss this further in chapter eight.

Angels help us in many ways and I will discuss more details on this a bit later. Unlike people, as soon as you ask angels for help, they will help you! They also will never judge you and are always supportive, even if you are acting less than saintly.

I ascribe to the belief that we are all connected, that we are not separate from God and the angels are part of God as well. We are all connected and one. You could compare all of the beings on the planet as part of a human body. In the body, there are cells, organs, and other parts that you can look at individually but combine to make the whole being. You might think of angels as being the ear of God and so while separate, the entire being of God receives information clearly from the angels.

There are many different types of angels, and there are three types that I will address in detail in this book. I think there are many more types of angels, but these are the types of angels that deal directly with human affairs and are easy for us to connect with. The first type of angel which I am sure most of you are familiar with is the guardian angel, the second is the specialty angel, and the third type is the Archangel. You can read specifically about each of these types of angels in the chapters dedicated to each in this book.

Angels come in so many types, shapes and sizes! They can be as different as you and I or as different as a frog and a horse. There are angels that feel male, that feel female, that are white in coloring, or purple. Some angels have black wings (this doesn't mean that they are dark or evil). There are also angels that have a light almost fairy-type of energy and those that are more serious. None of them are better than their peers, they are just different. I also believe that angels will appear to us in a way that makes sense in our cultural context and that is not intimidating to us. If you expect the angel to be male, the angel will likely appear male even if the true nature of that angel is androgynous or female in energy.

Many people describe their loved ones who have crossed over as being their guardian angel. Many times loved ones who have passed can act like a guardian angel in that they watch out for us and give us guidance and assistance. Generally speaking though, angels are a different type of being than humans or animals. There are angels, however, who have chosen to incarnate and have a human life for one reason or another, so this is not a hard and fast rule. There are complexities about this that I am still trying to learn and understand.

Angels Throughout the World and in History

I want to emphasize that angels are not exclusive to one religion. Many religions in the world talk about angels: Christianity, Islam, and Judaism, just to name a few. It is my opinion that these world religions have all explained angels from their cultural contexts but the angels are there regardless of our beliefs. It makes sense that all these cultures have written about angels because angels are always there. Many angel names end in "el" which means "of God" because one of their main roles is to act as intermediaries between us and spirit or the creator in order to help answer our prayers.

Angelology

Some may be surprised to learn that there is a field of study called Angelology, or the study of angels. I will go only briefly into this because the main purpose of this book is to give basic information on angels and how we can work with them. It should be noted however that there are those who study and who have studied angels in an academic sense for centuries. There are several books listed at the back of the book which can provide a more academic approach to angels should you choose to investigate. The word angelology comes from the Greek words 'logos' for word and 'angelos' for angel and is the study of angels.

Angelic Orders

Pseudo Dionysius, the Areopagite (a member of a tribune in Athens, Greece) was a philosopher and Christian mystic who created the Celestial Hierarchy. The hierarchy classifies the angels into specific ranks and orders which relate to the duties of that particular angel type. This hierarchy has been referred to in the centuries since as a way to categorize angels and understand their purpose and areas of specialty. There are many free copies of this available online if you would like to read it for yourself, however, I have listed the hierarchy below and summarized the information below for your reference. The Celestial Hierarchy lists 9 orders of angels which are classified in three choirs.

First Choir	Second Choir	Third Choir
1) Seraphim	4) Dominations	7) Principalities
2) Cherubim	5) Virtues	8) Archangels
3) Thrones	6) Powers	9) Angels

Each angel order has different qualities and areas that they focus on. I will share a brief description below of each order so that you get a sense of their purpose and characteristics. Again if you want to know more, you can read more in the Celestial Hierarchy and some of the other books listed in the sources.

Seraphim: The name Seraphim means the burning ones. The Ethiopian, Greek, and Hebrew words for Seraphim, translate as serpent, snake, or dragon. The Seraphim are mentioned in the Old Testament (Hebrew Bible) in the apocryphal *Book of Enoch*. They are said to emit love and a light so bright that no being can see them and to have 6 wings. It is said that four Seraphim surround God and they burn from love.

Cherubim – The Cherubim are described in the Old Testament many times. They are said to have guarded the Tree of Life in Eden with a flaming sword. They are described as having four faces; one of a bull, a human, a lion, and lastly that of an eagle. They have wings which can be heard from afar and also have wheels on their bodies. Most people think of Putti or small baby-like angels when they think of Cherubim but their description in actual texts is nothing like the babies at all.

Thrones (also called the Ophanim by some) – The Thrones are described as being a wheel within a wheel, covered with eyes, and emanating light.

Dominations (also called Dominions) – The Dominations are said to rule over the lower orders and that they receive their guidance from the Seraphim and Cherubim. They work on the cosmic level and, therefore, are rarely revealed to people. They are reported to look like humans with feathered wings and look much like angels depicted in artworks, though they are armed with balls of lights which are attached to their swords or scepters.

Virtues – The name Virtues is connected to the Greek term for might. Their key responsibility it to oversee the movement of the heavens.

Powers – The Powers angels, sometimes called the authorities, work with the Principalities. They are warrior angels and are said to act as an elite guard against dark forces. They oversee the distribution of power amongst humans. They also oversee the balance of the light and dark on earth, watch over the celestial paths between the material world and heaven, ensuring that all souls who leave the mortal plane reach heaven safely. Some say this order is more likely to fall from grace while others say this order never does.

Principalities – (Called Archai by some) The Principalities or Rulers work with the Powers angels. They bear crowns and carry scepters and they give blessings to the material world. They inspire people in the realms of art and science and are educators.

Archangels – The word Archangel is from the Greek word for Chief Angel and is used in the New Testament. There is some disagreement about the number of Archangels. Only Michael is specifically named in the canon (official church doctrine) as an Archangel. There is also some disagreement about whether there might be a difference between Archangel the order and Archangel, angel above all angels. The first can denote the class just above angels while the latter can indicate the highest of all angels who is believed to be Michael.

Angels – The word angel means messenger in Greek. They are the lowest order of the angels and the ones that work the most with humans and other living beings. They are said to act as messengers between humans and the heavens and the creator.

It should be noted that there are several people who have re-categorized the hierarchy or created their own over the centuries including Saint Thomas Aquinas, Saint Ambrose, Saint Jerome, and others. I share this celestial hierarchy as an example only. This is simply one description and I encourage everyone to follow what resonates for them.

THREE

Guardian Angels

Angels are everywhere around us and each of us has at least one angel assigned to us from birth to assist and comfort us. So though we may feel alone, we never truly are. Our guardian angels are always communicating with us and helping to answer our prayers. When we learn how to listen to them, it is amazing to discover how often they are sending us messages of love, support, and guidance!

Guardian angels know you well and are excellent for providing comfort in times of stress. If you are sensitive, you might even feel them playing with your hair or touching your shoulder and back to comfort you. They express only love. While it might feel like an invasion of privacy to know that they are with us in our most intimate moments, just know that they do not judge us. I believe that often our need for privacy comes from a sense that we will be judged for what we are doing. Because guardian angels *do* know us so well, they are excellent angels to ask for guidance. They know our deepest desires and also our greatest dreams. Know that you can ask your guardian angel for suggestions and assistance at any time and they will help you! Our thoughts and feelings are like instant prayers to the universe so when you need help, just think to yourself, "angels, please help me with (insert your request here)." I will go into more details on how to ask for and receive help a bit later too.

Guardian angels are assigned to us at birth and for many of us even before that! They are always by our side providing comfort, guidance, and assistance. No two guardian angels are alike, just like no two people are alike. In my experience, the type of guardian angel we have correlates to our personality, what we need help with, and what our mission is in this life. While angels don't have a gender in the way that we do, they can have a more female or male energy.

My mother's guardian angel for example is male, looks African or African-American, has dread locks and plays the bass (my mother is a bass player). He wears funky clothes and often appears on the hood of my mom's car to get her safely to and from work on her long drives. He totally suits my mom since he is also a musician, and is also clearly a non-conformist like my mother. It probably sounds funny to think about an angel like this but angels really are different from each other as we can be from each other. There are also some angels that resemble angels depicted in classical paintings and some that are very colorful or seem almost alien in appearance. Know that your guardian angel was chosen just for you and is a perfect fit, regardless of what he or she looks like.

If you would like to connect with your guardian angel, invite them to make their presence known. Sit or lie down in a quiet and peaceful place and see if you receive any impressions. You might feel something, hear a word, or feel a light touch. Pay attention to any sensations you receive.

While you are doing this meditation, you may hear their name or hear it in your mind as if it is your thought. Keep in mind that angels may have common human names like "Bob" or they may have an angelic sounding name. I am told that they may also have more than one name. While it is nice to have their name, the important thing for us is our connection with them. If you do not know your angel's name but would still like to connect, you can simply choose a name for your angel. You can think of it as a nickname for them if that helps. When you say that name, simply imagine your angel is there and feel that connection.

Your angel will be so happy that you have reached out to connect with them. Since your guardian angel knows every detail of your life intimately, they are an excellent angel to call on for help. You can do this out loud, in your mind, or by visualizing the request or writing it down. Our guardian angels often watch us struggle because we simply haven't opened the door to their help by asking for it. Our lives here on planet earth are an experience in free will: we can choose to do things on our own, much like a child might say to his or her mother, "I can do this on my own," or we can ask for help. I see no reason not to ask for help. Asking the angels for assistance allows them to intervene on our behalf which can lead to a much easier, less stressful life. Not only do they help alleviate stress but they help things happen almost magically. This is because they are working on an energetic level and everything happens first on an energetic level and then manifests in the physical plane. If you are trying to do everything on a physical level, it is going to take longer and feel harder than if you change the energy first.

Working on the physical plane exclusively is kind of like working from the outside in. One analogy would be to look at an allergic reaction. If you get a hive, it might feel good to put some ointment on it to relieve the itching, and it will probably help; however stopping your body from reacting from the inside is going to be much more effective and faster. That is how angels work; they work with energy, which then takes shape in the physical world. It is always faster and more effective to work on the energetic level first or to work from the inside out and not the other way around. That is how guardian angels and other types of angels can get things to change so quickly and easily.

FOUR

Specialty Angels

First of all, let me just say that specialty angels are so incredible to work with! Just as people have specialties in terms of expertise and work, so do angels. This is a powerful piece of knowledge because it means that all you need to do is ask the angel in charge of whatever you need help with to help you.

For example, I asked the technology angels to help me recently. One week before my two year warranty on my kindle expired, my battery started not holding a charge. This proved to be a blessing in disguise because I was sent a brand new, improved model, for free! A similar thing happened with my camera! My camera lens stopped working with one week left on the warranty. I sent it back in and I was sent a brand new one for free. On top of that I sold my old camera battery and accessories for $20 and made a profit.

One of my favorite experiences with specialty angels happened when I called on the publicity angels to help me. I asked a friend if I could do readings at her coffee shop and she said yes, so a week or so later I planned to have my first night there. I had put a flier up in the coffee shop window about the readings and that was the only marketing I did. The afternoon before my first reading, the managing editor of the local paper called to ask if he could do a story on me. It was a lovely article and appeared in the paper just two days after my first night doing readings. Immediately my phone was ringing from people who had read the article and wanted to book a reading. It was such an amazing blessing and I never sent out a press release or called a reporter. I didn't even send an email to all my contacts letting them know I was giving readings there. This is how I know the angels helped me, it seemed magical and the effect on my life was immediate. So ask the specialty angels to help you and then have patience and see how it plays out.

As I was building my business, I asked the health care angels and the body care and wellness angels to help me because I was working really hard and struggled with finding enough money to pay for services that would help me relax and take care of my physical self. I went through a particularly lucky period in which I won door prizes for massages, facials, and other relaxing and health inducing treatments. I knew that this was, in large part, due to their assistance. I knew that in the future I would be able to pay for these services but while I was building my business, all my money and time as going back into the business and for necessities. To win free services was incredibly helpful, as I was often working 12 hours a day or more to establish myself.

You can ask the specialty angels to help you with big and small things. Since the angels are playful, the things you ask for help with do not need to be serious. An example of calling on the specialty angels for something fun happened to me when I entered a hat contest at a night club. I was wearing a fascinator (a hat made mostly of feathers), a bright red dress, faux fur cropped jacket, and stiletto heels. I was dressed to the nines but still the competition was fierce. I got called up on stage as one of the finalists. I assessed the other competitors and saw that one of the women there had a beautiful, one-of a kind hat. I had a feeling that her hat should win over mine because it was more elaborate. I asked the winning angels and the confidence angels to help me with the contest if it was for the highest good. All the contestants had to walk on the stage in front of the hundreds of people in the crowd and the winner was chosen by applause. As I walked across the stage, the crowd clapped and hollered loudly. I later learned that one of my friends had run into a large group of her friends immediately before I walked across the stage and had asked them to clap for me. Since the timing was so perfect, I knew that the angels helped me at just the right moment. I received second prize, and the woman with the really elaborate hat won the grand prize. I went home that night with the $100 in my pocket for second prize and felt grateful that the angels had helped me even with this fun activity!

I had an incredible experience with the real estate angels when I was looking to rent an office for my business. I was getting busier and had been previously seeing clients at my home and local coffee shops but wanted a place that was energetically protected and private to do my work. I asked the real estate angels to help and started looking on a Tuesday. On Wednesday I found the perfect place, Friday I signed the lease, and a week later I had an open house. This had all the signs of angelic intervention: it was easy, fast, and perfect for me in every way! The office was very inexpensive (so low in fact that I wondered if it was a typo when I saw the monthly rate), it was 8 blocks from my house, it had brand new paint and carpet, it was quiet, and it was only the second office I looked at. Angelic assistance almost always makes me want to pinch myself to see if I'm dreaming because the outcome is better that I could even have imagined.

One of the best parts of this is that there are specialty angels for just about any type of assistance you can think of and all you have to do to receive their help is ask! This means there are housekeeping angels (some of my favorites), roofing angels, sewing angels, driving angels, carpentry angels, homework angels, dog-sitter angels, confidence angels, love angels, musical angels, plumbing angels, reading angels, writing angels, abundance angels, health angels, etc.! Let your imagination run wild and invite them into your life to help you and you could be amazed at the results that you have. The specialty angels have literally changed my life and I know they would love to help you.

You can recognize their assistance when things fall into place incredibly easily and with very little effort on your end. In all of the examples I listed, I did very little to elicit the benefits but mentally ask for their help. In the case of the newspaper article, I didn't hire a publicist, write a press release, or do much at all to market myself or the readings I was doing. Normally getting press would involve all or some of these steps and I didn't do any of them. The angels connected me with just the right person at just the right time to help me. It is always nice to remember to thank the angels when they help you since they like to be thanked, just like people do.

My immediate family has shared in some amazing experiences with specialty angels as well. My step-dad has a hauling and moving business, which means he often ends up with items that people are getting rid of which have value but he does not want or need. In one particularly impressive example, he had some metal siding that he'd been holding onto for years and in asking the finder angels to connect him with the right buyer, he posted the siding on craigslist (something he had done several times before). He sold the siding a few days later for $1700, not only was he richer, but he had more space and the buyer was happy to have the siding!

If you want to you can take a moment right now to think of something that you could use help with. It can be anything practical or whimsical and ask the angels in charge of that to help you. Be patient and don't be surprised if what you wish for happens faster than you could have imagined.

FIVE

Archangels

Archangels are a powerful type of angel so I am dedicating a whole chapter on them because they can be extremely effective angels to call on. They are the only angels specifically listed in the Bible and in many religious texts. Each Archangel is believed to have a specific role and specialty so that you may call on specific Archangels for assistance in various areas of your life. Often an Archangel will make itself known to a person who has a life mission in the particular area the Archangel assists with.

The number of Archangels known and named in various cultures varies from 4 to 12 or more. I believe there are more that we may not know about.

Archangels are a very powerful type of angel, likened to the commanders of armies of angels. They are mentioned specifically in the Christian Bible, the Koran, and the Jewish Torah or Old Testament. Aside from guardian angels, they are probably the most well-known type of angels. So if you are working with or asking for help from an Archangel, know that you are also working with a lot of other angels as well. Archangels are similar to specialty angels in that they have specialty areas or expertise but they often have more than one area they can help us with, unlike specialty angels. For example, Archangel Chamuel specializes in clearing dark energy, finding romance, life purpose, and also finding lost items. He is a very handy angel to know! There are lots and lots of Archangels (I can't tell you exactly how many) so I will just list some of the ones that I work with and am familiar with. Here is a little bit of information on each Archangel:

Michael the Archangel or Saint Michael is a powerful protector and warrior. He is said to have led the battle against the army of fallen angels and he is often depicted in artwork slaying the devil. His name means "Power of God" and he is indeed powerful! He can help if you feel fearful and he can protect you against real or imagined fears. For this reason, he is a great protector for the military and law enforcement. He was named a saint by the Catholic Church so you may see him referred to as Saint Michael even though he is an angel. He also is great for clearing dark energies and energetic cords (connections between people that transmit energies and emotions). Archangel Michael can also help you with your life mission. He is there to help many of us who have a life-purpose that involves working in light-energy and shifting paradigms to the new way of life and business. He is usually the first angel I call on when I need assistance of any kind.

Gabriel is mentioned in the Christian Bible as the angel who came to Mary and announced that she would give birth to Jesus. Gabriel acts as a main messenger between us and heaven, and helps us with anything to do with communication: whether it is talking, singing, writing, or even body-language! Call on Gabriel whenever you need help with any type of communication or with having confidence in your communication.

Raphael is an angel who helps with a whole host of issues. While he is not in the Catholic canon (approved religious text), he is mentioned in the *Book of Tobit*. In this story, Raphael plays a great role in many different ways. In the *Book of Tobit* (an apocryphal book of the bible), he helped heal a blind man, restored a family's fortune, played matchmaker, released demons from a young woman, and helped a traveler travel safely. This is an angel who has a great sense of humor! Call on Raphael for assistance in romance, traveling, healing, and chance meetings. His name means "Healer of God", but he doesn't heal just the physical so call on him for help with love, health, safe travelling, chance meetings, and clearing dark energies. He is one of my go-to angels.

Uriel is the Archangel that is often described as the counselor angel. Uriel means "Light of God" which makes sense when you think of clearing dark emotions and going into the light. He helps us deal with emotions and clear out toxic emotions and relationships. He also helps with extreme weather and natural disasters. Call on Uriel for help with relationships, weather related problems (especially wind), and clearing emotions and beliefs that are no longer serving you.

Chamuel is a multi-talented Archangel who can help with romance, clearing dark and negative energy, life-purpose, and also finding lost items. He is a very powerful Archangel and I call on him often. His name means "He who seeks God." Call on Archangel Chamuel for assistance with finding anything that you want in your life, including love, and clearing anything you don't want in your life such as ghosts and entity attachments. He is incredible with finding lost items such as wedding rings!

Jophiel is a beautiful Archangel whose name means "Beauty of God" and she does have beautiful energy! She has a more feminine energy than many of the other Archangels and can help beautify or uplift anything in your life including your thoughts, emotions, your physical space, etc. She works a lot with people who do some kind of design work such as stylists, designers, decorators and artists. Call on her if you need beauty in any area of your life (even a new hairstyle!) and you may be amazed at the results.

Ariel is a wonderful angel to work with for tapping into nature cycles and for working with animals. Ariel means "Lion of God" and she is a strong force! Think of our associations with lion and you will have a sense of her – strong, dignified, and unfazed. Ariel can help us when working with the nature spirits, plants, animals, and the environment. Call on her for help in any of these areas and when you need to feel more strength and dignity, regardless of external circumstances.

Haniel can help us tap into moon energy and feminine energy and intuitive knowing. Haniel means "Glory of God" and is a powerful but gentle angel who can help with clairvoyance, divine timing and connecting with feminine energy. Haniel is associated with the planet Venus and can also help with love, companionship, and connection.

Zadkiel can help us with letting go and forgiving. His name means "Righteousness of God" and he is a fantastic angel for helping release judgment and blame and to replace these feelings with mercy and empathy. He can help heal relationships and also help us forgive people (even ourselves).

Sandalphon is the brother of Metatron and one of the only two Archangels believed to have had a human life. He is said to help transport our prayers to God. He works through music and is believed to be the guardian of the earth. He also helps fight against dark forces and reestablish harmony. He is said to determine the gender of a child in the embryo stage so you can call on him to determine the gender of your baby.

Metatron is the brother of Sandalphon and the other Archangel who is believed to have had a human life. He is described as God's mediator with men. He is believed to keep the records of men (the Akashic Records). He works a lot with children. He can also assist people in crossing over into the after-life.

Azrael is the Archangel that helps us with life changes and life-transitions of all kinds. His name means "Angel of Death" which might sound scary, but he is here to help ease a transition from one form of being to another. He is an excellent angel to call on if you are helping a loved one transition to the other side, bringing a child into this world, making a career change, and any big transition in life. He helps us go through the transition more smoothly and will also guide us to make changes if they help us in the long run.

Raguel helps us build and maintain harmony in relationships. You might think of him as a mediator. He can also help you if you need to go to court or resolve a conflict with someone.

Raziel helps us work with anything esoteric. Raziel means "Secrets of God," so you can ask Raziel to help you with anything that is complex or tough to understand, especially of a spiritual nature. If you are trying to deepen your spiritual understanding, studying something challenging or working on manifesting, ask Raziel to help you.

The Archangels are excellent allies and I encourage you to call on those whose names and descriptions resonate for you. I feel a very strong connection with Archangel Michael. I first realized this connection when I was at the Isabella Gardner Stewart Museum in Boston and saw an incredible painting from across the room. The painting was titled *Archangel Michael* and showed Archangel Michael sitting on a throne. He was wearing armor and had a sword which he was using to keep a demon or devil at bay. The strange thing is that when I looked at the painting, I experienced a feeling of recognition as if I knew him! If you are drawn to one of these angel names or descriptions, you may have a connection to that angel.

I realized years later that I have the female version of Michael, or Michelle, as my middle name. My name shows some of my connection with the angelic realm. My middle name shows my connection to Michael and my last name is Powers which is one of the orders of angels! As I worked as a medium and angel communicator, I realized that one of my missions in life is to help people learn about and connect with angels and it is no surprise – it is right in my name. This could be the name you were given at birth or the name you have now, both are significant. It doesn't mean that you don't have a connection with angels if you don't have an angel name, but if you do have an angel name, it is good to pay special attention as you are likely meant to work closely with that angel or angels.

Those of us who do have a connection with an Archangel often have a life purpose or mission that has something to do with that Archangel's specialty. A life mission is something our soul came into this life to do. It is something significant and usually extends much beyond ourselves and usually has to do with helping people or the planet in some way. Our life mission may be very different from what we are doing in our life right now. If you would like more information on your life mission, ask the Archangels to send you signs and guidance to help you understand what you came here to do.

It is also fun to see how the angels send you people with their names to let you know they are helping you. There are so many examples of this that I can't share them all. One great occurrence of this happened when my friend Jan and I were leaving West Hollywood after a fabulous trip there. We had called a limo to take us to the Burbank airport as it was a very early flight. I always call on Archangel Raphael when I travel for safety and ease of traveling. When our limo driver pulled up, the driver's name was Rafael! I laughed and smiled to myself and knew that we were protected on our journey. We arrived in no time at the airport and upon checking in learned that our flight had been cancelled because the plane had been struck by lightning not once but twice, as it descended! We were rerouted through San Francisco and everything went smoothly, but I was so glad the angels sent me a sign of protection and support through the name of our limo driver. I thanked them for keeping us safe on our journey.

I call on Archangel Michael for help all the time for various things, and this proved fortuitous on a trip to Las Vegas. I went with a friend to attend the Consumer Electronics Show and the town was packed. We walked out of our hotel to get a taxi and the line for a cab was about 10 people long. We needed to meet our friends for dinner and were concerned about being late. I asked Michael to help and as we turned and walked just around the corner, a cab was dropping off some customers, right in front of us. We hopped into the cab with no wait, and the cab driver was a hilarious Croatian who could have been a stand-up comic. It was an entertaining and fast ride to our dinner, and we arrived on time. I asked the driver for his name and was not too surprised when he said Mike, or the shortened version of Michael. I thanked Michael for helping us and I am sure he was with us the rest of the evening because everything continued to flow easily.

There are many forms of the name Michael, for example, the Spanish version is Miguel. Another example of variations on an Archangel name is Gabe or Gabby instead of Gabriel. If you pay attention to people's names, you can often get a sense of who their angels are and if you keep meeting a ton of Michaels or Raphaels – there is a good chance that angel is saying hello.

P.S. When you call on the Archangels, be ready for big shifts because they can make incredible things happen!

SIX

An Angel is Near

By now you know a lot about angels and if you haven't already felt their presence, you likely will soon. Since most of us can't see or hear the angels with our eyes and ears, the angels show us their presence in many different ways. I've had many clients ask me why we can't see angels with our eyes and one theory is that their power and beauty is so magnificent that it would overwhelm us. I have had the honor of seeing angels with my physical eyes (and not just my third eye) just a few times for a brief moment and they were amazing. They looked like energy in motion with flashes of light (imagine a moving prism). While seeing an angel is incredible, you don't need to have clairvoyance to experience their presence. I've listed several signs that can indicate an angel is near.

Recognizing the presence of an angel

When an angel or many angels are nearby you may notice many different signs and these are just some of the signs. Keep in mind that you might see an indication of their presence, or you might hear or feel them. Pay attention to all of your senses and don't exclude anything as trivial. Pay attention to anything that feels significant or recurring themes and messages. Our angels are constantly communicating and showing their presence. It is incredible how much and how often they communicate and once you recognize the signs you may be shocked. Below are some signs that an angel is near:

- An incredible feeling of overwhelming love
- Pressure changes in the air which make your ears pop
- A ringing sound in your ears
- A warmth coming from no apparent source
- The feeling of someone lightly brushing or touching your head, neck, back, or shoulders
- The sound of heavenly sounding music or bells
- The sound of wings beating
- Finding feathers in unusual places
- Seeing angel wings or an angelic being in the clouds

- Feeling like you are being gently hugged by wings that come from behind and envelop you
- Seeing "angel lights" or sparkling colored lights that have no apparent source
- Feeling and hearing a humming or vibration that encompasses you
- Finding coins or money
- Seeing rainbows

These signs may manifest in the physical: you might find real feathers, or you might see something with a feather image on it. Both are valid indicators that an angel is showing their presence. You might also hear a reference to an angel or a song comes on that has the word angel in it. The song "Send me an Angel" *by Real Life* will often come on when I sense an angel nearby and am comforted by the message. When I hear that song, I also feel they are communicating that it would be a good time to ask for their help.

I experience these signs regularly and I expect that they are communicating with you as well, but it is highly likely that you may not have recognized some of these signs. In the first chapter, I mention my first angelic experience in which I heard the sound of wings beating, feeling surrounded by love, and being surrounded by a humming and vibration. This was an extreme example, as

I experienced many of these signs at once. The angels may give you just one sign, but that doesn't mean that their presence is any less significant.

Another favorite example of angels showing me a sign of their presence happened at a meeting. I was at a film networking event that I'd felt compelled to go to. It was an event in which filmmakers networked with other filmmakers and those who wanted to be involved in film. I was there with my good friend and confidante Jan, who also managed the video for my television show *Healing Powers TV*. The meeting had been happening for about 30 minutes in a closed room with no doors or windows to the outside. There was only one internal door which was several feet behind me. I couldn't believe my eyes when I looked up and saw a tiny, white feather floating from the ceiling. Since there were no birds in the room and no windows or vents through which the feather could have blown in, I knew that this was a sign from the angels. I pointed it out to Jan and we laughed out loud which disrupted the meeting.

After the meeting, I approached the organizers and asked about auditioning for one of the parts they had been discussing during the meeting. It was a role that was written as a male but was not gender specific. I auditioned and though they did cast a man in the role, they wrote in a part and asked me to do it since I'd auditioned and they felt they knew me. Since I had seen the feather, I knew that the angels were supporting me. That role later led to many great things acting-wise and I met some wonderful friends as well.

Another fun example happened when I had a television interview scheduled with Dr. Steven Farmer who was promoting his new book and discussing his work with animal spirit guides at the International New Age Trade Show (INATS). INATS is a large tradeshow held in a merchandise mart and Dr. Farmer had gotten my crew and me guest passes into the event. We were searching for a good place to do the shoot that would be quiet and where we'd be uninterrupted. We'd looked at several possible locations and walked to a room on the outskirts of the expo hall, a room that was quieter than the other locations and had a nice background.

Just prior to the meeting with Dr. Farmer, my good friend and videographer said that she felt it would be good to have a crystal to help protect the shoots from energetic intrusion. We walked into the room, listened and looked quickly and determined it was the best location and walked back out. Both Jan and I spotted something on the floor not far from the door to the room we were going to use. It was a $10 bill and it had not been there only moments before. This was also a place where there was not much foot traffic so it was rather surprising to find it there. Both Jan and I felt that it was a present from the angels for a crystal.

The interview with Dr. Farmer went very smoothly and afterwards Jan and I walked around to explore and also find the crystal we were meant to have. I felt that the crystal would be exactly $10. There were many, many vendors but we walked until I felt drawn to a particular area. I felt the urge to stop as we got close to a display of quartz crystals and I was amazed to see that there was one particular crystal I was drawn to. Jan felt the same about this particular crystal but it was quite large so I approached the vendor and asked how much it cost. He weighed the crystal and even though the price that showed on the scale was $10.25 the vendor told me $10 even. I paid for the crystal and thanked the angels for the gift to purchase the crystal and also for their help finding it. I feel that we were meant to have that crystal and I knew that the angels were there with us that day because we found just the right amount of money.

The angels can help with seemingly small or bigger problems or life areas. In fact I don't believe that there are even big or small problems for the angels, it is all just energy to them. I'll give another example of help that I think was on a much larger scale.

The worst shooting of its kind in history happened in July 2012 in Aurora, Colorado when an armed gunman entered a movie theater at a midnight showing of *The Dark Knight Rises*, and started shooting people in the theater. ABC News described it as the worst shooting in history with 71 people shot in just a few minutes. Twelve were killed and 58 others were shot and injured in this tragedy in which unsuspecting movie goers were targeted. The rampage caught everyone off guard and left the city of Aurora in a state of shock. At the time of the shooting, I lived less than 30 miles from the theater and I had several connections to people who were there or had planned to go and cancelled at the last minute.

This was a devastating shooting in which the gunman, a 24 year old former graduate student, armed himself and opened fire on the audience. The number injured and killed is astounding. As details about the evening were revealed, it became clear that it was incredible that more hadn't been killed. Colorado Governor John Hickenlooper stated, "What a miracle it wasn't worse." It was estimated that police arrived 60-90 seconds after the shooting started and the ambulance arrived just two and a half minutes after the shooter started which is incredibly quickly. Additionally, the shooter's semi-automatic rifle jammed during the attack which led to his being captured alive, and surely reduced the number of victims. I am not trying to minimize the trauma and tragedy people there experienced that night - I know what those at the theater experienced must have felt like a nightmare come to life. I do think it could have been even worse than it was.

A few days after the shooting, a vigil was held at the theater and many attended to give their support and pray for the victims. Crystal Fuller was there and took a photo of the gathering. After she posted it online, a friend stated that she could see an angel in the clouds. I've included the photo below so you can decide for yourself. It certainly looks to me like an angel was watching over the vigil. So many people were there praying for the victims of the theater so it would not surprise me if an angel, or many angels were there.

Photographed by Crystal Fuller. Source: *The Denver Channel*

Note: *If you are viewing this in black and white, the angel is not as visible. Go to the Denver Channel website (website found in the sources) to view in color.*

SEVEN

How Angels Communicate with Us

One of the most common questions I get is about how angels communicate with us. First I'd like to share that sometimes angels do communicate with us directly in ways that we can perceive but not everyone has the ability to receive this communication directly. Those with special "clair" gifts may be able to receive this kind of communication directly. "Clair" means clear, and when connected with another word like seeing, means clear-seeing. Someone who is clairvoyant or clear-seeing can see the spiritual world. There are some for whom these gifts are more pronounced than for others. The same is true for our physical senses. For example, most people can hear well but some are hard of hearing and others are tone deaf whereas some people have very sensitive hearing. I bring this up because many people dismiss their own clair-senses if they are subtle. Clair-senses include clairvoyance (seeing), clairaudience (hearing), clairalience (smelling), clairsensience (feeling), and claircognizance (knowing). If you are gifted in one of these ways, you might actually see, hear, feel, smell, or simply know that an angel is near and that they are communicating with you. Bear in mind that these senses are usually more subtle then our physical ones. When I see clairvoyantly or with my third eye, the image is usually hazier and less defined then when I see with my physical eyes. That doesn't mean it isn't there but our clair-senses may feel very different from our physical ones. When we are sensing some of the signs mentioned in the previous chapter, it may mean that we have a gift in one of these areas. If you feel you do, this is something worth developing. There are classes and telecourses you can take from just about anywhere in the world as long as you have a phone or internet connection. Follow your intuition to learn about and develop these and ask your angels for guidance with this.

Because angels are on a different energetic vibration, it can sometimes be challenging to communicate with them directly. Angels are always sending us messages through our environment and also through our thoughts and intuition. For every message we receive from them, I have been told that they have sent the message 100 times. As soon as we know how they communicate with us, we can more easily follow their guidance which is often an answer to our prayers, hopes, and dreams!

Messages in Music

One of the favored ways the angels communicate with us is through music. Sometimes the name of the song, the artist, or the lyrics will be significant. I mentioned the example before about hearing the song "Send Me an Angel," but the messages can be varied. One of my favorite ways to receive guidance is to ask a question, ask the angels for protection, and then turn on the radio or the mp3 player on shuffle and see what comes up. It is amazing how often the songs provide exactly the guidance I need.

Keep in mind that you do not necessarily need to hear the music in order to receive a message that way. Once when I was travelling in China, I wanted to attend a music festival in Beijing but none of my friends could attend with me. I was unsure whether to go on my own, and if I did go, how to travel there. I had been looking into different options and debating whether to go at all. The song "Angel" by Sarah McLachlan popped into my head. At one point in the song, the lyrics state, "fly away in the arms of an angel," and this was the part of the song that remained in my head. I knew it was a message from the angels and when a friend offered to help me book a plane ticket through a local travel agent without asking, I knew it was meant to be.

The trip was indeed magical and I met wonderful people and had a fantastic time. The event was a Mongolian Folk Punk Festival outside the city, not an event that most expats would attend. When I received the message from the angels, I knew I would be safe and provided for. Sure enough, the first night I was in Beijing before the festival started, I met a business man who was in Beijing on business and was fluent in both Chinese and English. I invited him to the festival and since he had finished with his work and wasn't leaving town for two days, he decided to join. During the festival we talked and walked around together. He acted as translator for me the entire time which was a great help since I only speak a handful of Mandarin words and phrases. He was also very gentlemanly and a nice conversation partner.

Not only was this man helpful at the festival but he had gotten vouchers from his hotel for free Thai massages and could only use one, so after standing all day at the festival, I went and had a two hour Thai massage for free! The next day he and I went to the Forbidden City (the Palaces of the Ming through the Qing dynasties) and to a fun street in Beijing with wild street food. Then we exchanged email addresses and said goodbye and parted ways. I think we both had a great time and helped each other out.

I know the angels helped me on this trip to make a connection and when the song suddenly popped into my head, it helped me to understand that if I went, I would be safe. When things happen easily and quickly, that is often a sign of help from the angels!

The angels can give us just the right uplifting message through music as well. There was a time when I felt that I had been working so hard and was tired and worn out. I asked the angels for a message and turned on my Pandora (an internet radio program) and the song "The Best is Yet to Come" performed by Michael Buble came on. It helped give me the confidence and comfort in the knowledge that things were moving in the right direction and not to give up hope.

Sometimes the messages can be quite literal (and funny too)! I got a very precise message through music once when a friend was coming over and I was tidying up my place and had the music on. Just then a song called "Turn it down" by Kaskade came on. I thought it might be a message so I turned down the music but not apparently enough because a short time later my friend called me from the front door. Apparently she was there and had knocked, but I couldn't hear. Thankfully it wasn't a problem but I always get a laugh when I think about that particular message in music.

Numbers

Another way that angels communicate with us is through repeated numbers. Numbers are said to have deep meaning through numerology as well as in science and mathematics. There certainly can be magic and deep meaning in numbers and if the angels know you are using a system to receive communication from them, they will make sure to use it!

I especially notice when the same number appears in a series like 333, 444, or 777. These numbers can appear anywhere, but common locations include license plates, email addresses, the number of emails in your inbox, license plates, digital clocks, dates, bank statements, receipts, register totals, and anywhere else where numbers are listed.

The number 444 in particular is a number that indicates divine blessings and protection and 333 is a sign of support and a very divine number. Ones represent new beginnings and direction and that our energy is being directed through our thoughts. If you see a lot of ones, make sure you are thinking positive thoughts and thinking about what you want to have and experience in your life. Twos are a sign that things are moving forward and can indicate progress and partnership. In my experience, fives indicate change and forward motion. Sixes represent partnership and union – think of honey combs and their hexagonal shape, they could not be made without teamwork! Sevens indicate angelic support and things moving in a positive direction. Eights indicate abundance and the everlasting loop of energy, time, money, love or whatever we desire. Again it is a good idea to think about positive things so that you are attracting an abundance of positive things your way. Nines represent completion and endings. When you see a lot of nines, it can be a sign that it is time to end one chapter of your life and start a new one.

I recommend the book *Angel Numbers 101: The Meaning of 111,123, 444, and Other Number Sequences,* by Doreen Virtue. In the book, she lists possible meanings for the numbers 1 through 999. I also recommend the website *What's Your Sign* by Avia Venefica for a listing of the symbolic meaning of numbers. You can find this listing at: http://www.whats-your-sign.com/spiritual-meaning-of-numbers.html. As with anything that you read, see if the meaning resonates for you. Just like dream interpretation, the meanings may vary from person to person, so if you read something that doesn't seem right, listen to your intuition.

Also bear in mind that if the angels know we are looking for signs in a particular way, they will communicate with us in that way.

Overheard Conversations

Another common way that angels send us messages is through overheard conversations. You could hear people at work, at a café, or in line at the grocery store (or anywhere really) and you might catch a name, a place, or an occupation. Again, if you have asked for a sign, pay attention to anything that is repeated or significant.

The individuals may be talking about the weather or the name of a book, or even about traffic or construction. Pay attention to anything that seems unusual or repeated and if you are unsure of the meaning, ask the angels to confirm, clarify or help you understand it. For example, I asked for signs when I was thinking of going to LA and was stunned by the sheer number of references to California and Los Angeles I heard in one day in conversations, song, movie and television references. Try it and pay attention to what you see and hear. You may be amazed!

Urge to do Something

One great form of communication we receive is an urge to do something, especially if it is automatic and there is no logical reason to do it. This could be guidance to bring you something you would like, to protect you, or to prevent something you don't want. One example that immediately comes to mind happened when I was in college. I was driving to Boulder from my hometown of Lafayette to pick up my driver's license and I always went on one main road to get there. That day I inexplicably started to go on a different road. I was so confused by this once I realized I was driving a different way that I literally turned around and started going the way I normally go. As I approached Boulder, I was pulled over for speeding and of course I didn't have my driver's license. I ended up with a hassling situation and a ticket I had to pay for! I am sure if I had gone the other way I wouldn't have gotten a ticket. This was before I was aware of how angels communicate with us. Even though this was an expensive experience, in a way it was worth it because it was such a clear demonstration of why it is a good idea to listen to our intuition.

Idea in Your Head

A similar form of communication happens when an idea pops into your head suddenly. The angels communicate with us through thoughts. They are pure energy so it is easy for them to communicate with direct intent. If you are clairaudient, you might hear what they say or you might just hear their thought in your mind as if it is your own. Some of us are so good at receiving that it can be difficult to tell what is your thought and what is someone else's. This is something I struggle with, however on the positive side, I do receive messages quite easily in this way from my angels. In particular this happens to me as I am drifting off to sleep and when I am in the bath or shower. I have learned to have a pen and notepad on my nightstand for this reason! Sometimes I am constantly turning the light on and off to jot things down that I know they are telling me.

Written Messages

Seeing written messages is a very clear way the angels communicate. You might see a message on a billboard, license plate, a newspaper headline, book cover, or even someone's t-shirt. Keep in mind, the angels often have a sense of humor about this. A friend of mine was contemplating leaving her job and wasn't sure if this was in her best interest and asked for a sign. Shortly thereafter she saw a bumper sticker that read "You have nothing to lose but your job." She promptly quit her job, easily found another and never regretted the decision.

I am often amazed at a quote I read that is just the perfect message I need to hear. You might read this quote anywhere. If you keep seeing quotes from a particular person, be open to the fact that the person who said it may be one of your spirit guides or that you would benefit from learning more about that person or their work. Einstein comes up a lot for me and I was surprised when I read how spiritual a person he was. He was brilliant scientist who was also very wise. He is often credited as saying, "Everybody is a genius. But if you judge a fish by its ability to climb a tree, it will live its whole life believing that it is stupid." If you are reading this quote right now, this is most likely a message for you!

Divination Tools

There are many great divination tools out there that you can use as a tool for communication. The word divination comes from the Latin word *divinaire* which means "to foresee, to be inspired by a god." Divination is a method of connecting with information from the divine. There are many methods or tools for divination that you may be familiar with: tea leaves, tarot cards, scrying (looking into a mirror or mirror-like surface to see a vision) runes, palm reading, pendulums, and many, many more. Oracle cards are one of my favorite tools and I do use them regularly for myself. It can be a great way to find out what your angels and spirit guides would like to communicate, either in general, or in response to a specific question. Just make sure to think about what you would like answered; if you are asking two questions at once you may get an unclear response. Also be sure to clear your card deck and ask the Archangels (especially Archangel Michael) for protection and assistance understanding the reading.

There are other divination tools too such as runes, the I-Ching, reading tea leaves or coffee grounds, palm reading, etc. There are many tools you can use to receive guidance. I encourage everyone to use whichever you feel drawn to and to ask your angels to help you find just the right method for you. For years, I was very drawn to various tarot decks and I bought several but none of them ever seemed right for me. I now know that part of reason I experienced this is that the intention of the creator influences the deck. You cannot clear this type of energy from a deck. There are some decks which have distinctly dark or sad energy, so I would not recommend using one of those decks for readings, as you will likely get sad or dark readings out of the deck.

Let your intuition guide you to the best deck for you and if a deck of cards or another divination method doesn't feel quite right, don't get that one and keep searching until one feels right. Also keep in mind that certain decks or tools are good for certain questions or at certain times. I have about 20 different decks and I choose a particular deck that I am drawn to at that particular moment. But don't feel like you need to buy a bunch at once, you can start out with one deck and get additional ones when you feel drawn to them!

Here is a summary of the ways in which angels send us messages and communicate with us:

- Messages in music
- Symbols
- Numbers
- Overheard conversations
- Unexplained urges to do something
- Idea that pops into your head
- A written message on a billboard, book cover, t-shirt, or newspaper article
- Divination tools such as oracle cards

How to Listen

One important thing to keep in mind with angels is that we need to be open, receptive, and paying attention in order to recognize that they are communicating. Also if our minds are busy, then we oftentimes cannot hear them, literally or figuratively. It is very difficult to both talk and listen at the same time – I am sure you would agree! When we are busy and literally talking, or when our mind is busy, we are essentially talking to them. The angels take our thoughts quite literally sometimes and bring us what we are thinking about. It is important for this reason to think about what

we want and also to make sure that we are not essentially talking to them all the time without ever listening.
A physical conversation would not get very far if we operated in this way. Most of us fill our schedules until we have little time to listen to our spirit guides' messages. If we have asked for guidance and assistance, we have started the conversation and we need to give them some time to respond. We can better receive their communications when we have quiet time. For some people meditating is a great tool, for others, taking a walk in nature is a great way to connect with them. I oftentimes get great responses from the angels when I am in the bath or the shower. Stopping and being receptive for as little as five minutes can help so don't feel like you have to have an hour to do this. Of course more time is great but since even a small tip from the angels can make a big difference, even a little receptive time can help. If taking five minutes of private quiet challenging, perhaps you can find a minute or two to step into the bathroom for some receptive time. Do whatever you can and by all means ask the angels to help you find the time for this communication!

If you feel you are getting guidance from the angels but aren't sure, you can ask for a clear sign and then pay attention. If you are still getting mixed messages it could be because the question is unclear or maybe you are conflicted about what you really want. It is best not to use the word "should" when asking for guidance because the word should assumes there is a right or a wrong answer. The angels do not want to interfere with our free will so it is best to ask the question in a different way.

I'll share an example of how clear the angels can be when you ask them! As I built my business, I felt that I was getting the guidance to increase my prices but I wasn't sure. As I was driving home one day, I asked the angels to send me a clear sign, a sign so clear that I could *not* misunderstand it. I asked the question out loud and in my mind and when I arrived at home, I checked my mail. There was a business magazine in my mailbox and the headline read, "Why you should raise your prices." Inside the magazine, the article with that title listed 10 reasons why prices should be raised. I thanked the angels for being so clear, raised my prices, and it was indeed the best thing for me and my business. This is just one example, so keep in mind that the sign could be something you read, something a friend mentions, a bumper sticker, or any number of signs listed above and other examples I haven't listed or thought of.

Another example of asking for clarification happened recently when I got the message to go to Estes Park. I had a women's weekend planned up in Estes so I asked the angels for clarification. Then I kept hearing Stanley and I realized that it was not the women's weekend but rather I was to go to the Stanley Hotel in Estes. I asked for more clarification and then a friend told me about The Stanley Film Festival, a horror film festival that was happening at the Stanley Hotel. Again I wanted to make sure I understood correctly, so I asked for a sign I could not misunderstand and that evening, I saw a man wearing a t-shirt from the movie, *The Shining*. I knew this was a sign that I was to go to the festival since the movie *The Shining* was inspired by the Stanley Hotel. Still I wanted information on what my purpose was for going so I asked for a sign about that – particularly I wondered whether my purpose involved film or ghosts. I turned on Pandora and laughed when the first song that came on was "Unchained Melody" by the Righteous Brothers. For those who don't know the song, it is the song that plays in the movie *Ghost* when Demi Moore's character is on the potter's wheel and the ghost of Patrick Swayze's character is with her. This was the perfect sign because it was from a movie about ghosts so I know my purpose involved both films and spirits.

Once I was in Estes, I realized that this was accurate, but I also received a surprise because Stanley had not only been a reference to the Stanley Hotel but also to Stanley Kubrick, who directed "The Shining" movie. His spirit came to me during the festival and I was able to channel messages from him that related to my work specifically. Of course it never would have occurred to me that Stanley Kubrick would have wanted to communicate with me! I loved that the "Stanley" message the angels sent me had two meanings for the location as well as a spirit that wanted to communicate with me and wanted me to go to the festival.

If you'd like additional information on asking for and receiving signs, then I recommend the book *Sacred Signs: See, Hear, and Believe Messages from the Universe* by Adrian Calabrese.

EIGHT

Calling on Your Angels

We have many guides and substantial potential assistance from the spirit realm, but the trick is to understand how to connect with all of this help. There are so many guides and angels and wonderful beings who want to help us if we ask! This chapter is dedicated to giving you tips on how to ask for and receive help.

Asking for help from spiritual beings may sound like a foreign concept, but if you think about it, Catholicism uses this concept through patron saints. A patron saint is a person who has gone through the process of being named a saint by the Catholic Church. Each saint is named the patron saint of a certain topic.

For example, Saint Lucy is the Patron Saint of eye ailments or blindness because she was blinded shortly before she was martyred. Those in the Catholic faith are taught to call on patron saints for help with particular life areas or struggles. This is brilliant but we don't have to be Catholic to benefit from this. We can call on the help of our own spirit guides, angels and the spirit of any person.

How to ask for help and guidance

The fabulous thing about asking for help and guidance from our spirit guides is that it is *so* easy to do! There is no right or wrong way to ask for help and guidance, though some methods may resonate more for you. There are several methods of asking for help and guidance. You may make the request in writing, out loud, or you can simply think it! You may even visualize your request if that feels better for you. If you want the angels to help you with finances, you may think to yourself, "Angels, please help me increase my income." You may write this same prayer, or say it out loud, or you can visualize the angels bringing you money. The way you do it doesn't matter as long as you do it! Just think/say/write, "please help me with _____."

This process is so simple that it may feel too easy to be true, but that is not the case. We are certainly raised to believe that life is hard, but I'd like people to know that it doesn't have to be. Our prayers are heard by our angels and spirit guides as soon as we say or think them and because they are not limited by the physical reality in the way that we are (or feel we are), it allows them to intervene very quickly on our behalf. In some cases, what we ask for can happen very quickly and other times it can take some patience, but the process is as easy as asking for help.

Writing It Down

Your thoughts are heard instantaneously, but sometimes it increases the power and speed of the request by making it out loud or in writing. Writing the request down can be very powerful because we have a record of it and I highly recommend that you date your request so that you can track it more easily. I have been amazed at how written prayers and goals can have startling impacts on my life! The first time I made a list of goals in several areas of my life (13 to be exact), I was amazed when several of my goals came true so quickly. These were goals I had made for the year and all of them had felt like stretch goals, or goals that would be difficult to achieve at the time. I now make it a point to put major life goals and requests for assistance in writing and regularly review and update them.

I believe one reason written prayers are answered quickly is that when we write down our prayer, we are likely to be more specific, whereas our thoughts can be quite general. Writing down our prayers and requests for help can also help clarify what our vision is both for ourselves and our angels.

Getting Specific

Asking for help, in general can be very powerful, but asking for specific help can be magical. I've had many magical experiences relating to asking for specific help and been amazed at how I received just what I asked for. Getting specific can help our angels understand just what it is that we are wanting. For example, you might pray for more money and you find a nickel on the ground. The angels might consider your prayer answered but this is probably not what you had in mind.

There are many examples I can think of, some of them small in scale and others large in scale. I received the message that I was meant to do Reiki healing. I had an office to do readings but I thought it was too small for a massage table and I felt that it would be difficult to do Reiki treatments there. I asked the angels to help me work out the logistics of doing this type of healing work and I heard that I could use a yoga mat with towels and a pillow. I got home that afternoon and my step-dad offered me a very nice, thick yoga mat, yoga towels and two nice pillows I could use. This happened within the period of a couple of hours!

In another example, a family member asked for between $6,000 and $7,500 income for bills that month, and he did receive just that amount. It is worth noting that prior to that, income and bill paying had been a struggle. How often could our struggles be prevented or minimized by asking for specific assistance? Also note that it is helpful to ask for want you want or more. Otherwise they may deliver exactly what you ask when really you would have preferred more.

The angels will help you but because we are constantly praying through our thoughts and beliefs, it can take time for great changes to occur. It may present a challenge for us to go from being in poverty to being a millionaire in a month, though even this is possible. Asking for big things and then giving them time to help you is a good tactic. Ask them to help shift your beliefs and then follow the guidance you receive to help with this. Sometimes your beliefs may start to shift automatically or you might feel guided to learn about techniques including tapping, the EMT (Emotional Freedom Technique), Access Consciousness (BARS method), EMDR (Eye Movement Desensitization & Reprocessing) therapy, past-life regression, hypnosis, affirmations, or other methods that will help you release old blocks, patterns and beliefs. Follow whatever feels right for you as different methods work for different people.

You can ask for help for relatively small and seemingly large goals as well. I recently asked the angels to get me a free drink or drinks at a bar and I did pay for my first drink but I didn't like it very much so the bartender offered to make me a different one. She accidentally made me a different drink than the one I had ordered so then she made me a third drink (the one I had asked for) and charged me for neither of them. Later that night, a nice man bought me a drink as well so I had an abundance of free drinks that evening. In fact I was offered several more drinks that I turned down since I don't drink that much! It made me laugh because I got the drinks in an unusual way and I knew the angels had helped me. I got the free drinks just as I had asked. Ask the angels for the things and experiences you would like, have faith, and then see what happens.

Asking Out Loud

Saying our requests out loud is very powerful as then we are saying and hearing our request at the same time. I've known friends who have recorded affirmations (positive statements stated in the present to assist with manifesting) in their own voice and have had incredible results. Of course you might not feel comfortable doing this in front of others, so in that case, simply give your requests for assistance through your thoughts.

Ask for Help Again and Again

Let me address the importance of repetition here. It might seem silly to ask for the same thing over and over again but it can be imperative. The reason this is important is that we are living a free will experience here on earth. You might ask what the heck this has to do with it? Everything! The important point to remember about free will is that we all have the right to change our mind. This is beautiful because today you might wish for Fred but then you kiss him and realize Fred really isn't for you.

There is no harm done in terms of free will because tomorrow you can wish for Alan, or even Jessica. The universe and our angels do not, and cannot, assume that we want the same thing that we did yesterday or even this morning. Hence the importance of asking for what we want, again and again until we receive it. You will probably feel like a broken record. Keep asking anyway. I try to get in the habit of asking for help in the morning when I wake up (get the ball rolling right away) throughout the day when I think about it, and before I go to sleep at night. This is critical, particularly if you are a worrier (I will go more into that later).

If you receive what you asked for, then please tell your angels thank you and follow it up by a request of assistance with something else. This is not greedy this is just practical. *You cannot ask for help too much*. Any limitations we think exist come from us, as limitations do not exist in the angelic realm. Almost anything is possible – seriously folks. One of my favorite quotes applies here. It is, "Impossible is just an opinion, nothing else," by the Chef Vikas Khanna. Whatever you believe is possible and asking the angels to help you lends even more power to it.

Ask for What you Really Want

When you ask for assistance and guidance, also ask for what you truly want. For example, you may want a beautiful abundant home and to get this in the traditional way you would need a lot of money but if you pray for the money, you are not praying for what you truly want. If you pray for a beautiful abundant home, the angels may deliver an amazing opportunity to house-sit for a long term while your good friends go live abroad for a year, for example. Pray and ask for what you truly desire. Too often, people pray for the money only. Don't get me wrong, money can be a great tool but it is a means to an end, not the end. This might seem like an obvious thing to do but sometimes what we think we want is not really what we truly want. For example, people often times want a lot of financial success. They believe that if they have more money, they will feel happier and more secure. The truth is that when income increases to more than $50,000/year, we do not automatically get any happier. This has actually been studied by many people: a 2010 study by Marist found that happiness did not automatically increase with income higher than $50,000. We ask for money because we really want to reduce stress, feel more secure, have more freedom and ultimately be happier. What if we asked the angels to help us feel happier and more secure? That might get us to what we are truly striving for even faster. Think about why you are asking for those things and then decide if you'd like to alter your request. Asking for a combination of material things, experiences, and feelings is a great place to start.

Also bear in mind that the angels might help you get your goals in unusual ways. You might get a job through a friend and skip the application process or someone might give you just the perfect pair of boots in your size and favorite color without you having to purchase them. These are some examples and being open to different ways of receiving other than how you would expect to receive. You might also find that the angels send you what you had asked for (think of the finding a nickel example) and if that happens, just refine your request and ask again. Think of it as placing an order with the universe. Every time we get something that is not quite what we asked for, we can refine our request to improve our results over time.

It may help to think about this process like going to a restaurant. If you were hungry and simply asked the waiter to, "Bring some food," the waiter could fulfill your request by bringing you a bowl of uncooked string beans.

I like string beans as much as the next person but that would probably not satisfy my taste-buds, or satiate my hunger. If you asked for steak and potatoes, you might get closer to what you'd like. To get even more specific, you might ask for filet mignon cooked medium rare with a side of béarnaise sauce, mashed potatoes with truffle sauce, and a spring salad. Imagine what would happen if you wanted filet mignon but when you placed your order you asked for "food." I doubt you would get the filet! Keep your orders with the universe clear and specific.

If you start to get specific, the angels will likely help you answer your own prayers by shifting your life to match the experiences you are requesting. You might get messages and feel urges to change careers, find new friends, relocate, and start or give up a hobby, refocus your life, etc. If you don't like where you are, know that your current life is a reflection of your previous thoughts, actions and beliefs and these can be changed so that future results improve. The angels are your allies in this process. If you are unsure what you'd like, ask for the things you think you are sure about. Then ask the angels to help you be happier, more peaceful, healthier, etc. They can help you make the changes that will lead you to those feelings.

What angels cannot do

Angels will help with just about anything. One of the only exceptions here is that they will not help you with something that interferes with someone else's free will or is harmful to another person. For example, if you ask the angels to help a certain person fall in love with you, that is against that person's free will and they cannot help you with that. Angels never do anything harmful to another being as angels are pure love. They are always waiting to help you, but because of free will, they cannot intervene unless they are asked to.

The free will concept is important when saying prayers for another person as well. Sometimes the soul of a person will make a decision that seems like a "bad" thing to us. For example, they might decide to have a terminal illness in order to learn or experience something through the illness. The individual may also make life choices that are not pre-planned by their higher self and are leading to drug addiction. While we might believe that the drug addiction is bad, it is their choice to live this way. When praying for someone else, it is always important to pray for whatever is for their highest good. You can also ask for any healing that will help the individual. I believe it is best to not be prescriptive with prayers for others since we do not know the whole story of why someone is experiencing what they are experiencing. This is a complex area. Asking the angels to help with whatever is the best for the individual takes our opinion out of the situation and still helps the individual you are praying for.

Sometimes we experience a challenge as a soul in this life for purposes of spiritual growth (it could be almost anything). Angels cannot change the outcome of this but they can help give us comfort.

What angels can help you with

Angels can help with almost anything, but here are some examples. Once again I will mention that we need to ask for help because of free will. The one exception to this is if we are going to die before it is our time, angels will intervene whether you ask them to or not. There are many incredible intervention stories in which angels step in and save the day. I will discuss these later in the book.

Examples of areas for which angels can help:

- Parking (seriously!)
- Helpful connections

- Healing
- Safety
- Finding lost items
- Love and romance
- Healing relationships
- Housing
- Transportation
- Shopping

I have had incredible luck with parking and I am sure that it is because I ask the angels for help with parking all the time. You can ask in the moment but if you give them a little bit of warning before you need the parking spot, it gives them a bit of time to line it up for you. Note that asking for help in advance is a good thing to do in general. I have had some incredibly lucky and perfectly timed parking spots even in situations where there were very few parking spots. Asking the angels for help in this arena is highly recommended.

Finding lost items is another wonderful way to utilize angelic assistance. In some cases, after asking for help with the lost item, an idea of where it might be may pop into your head. Do not be too surprised if you find the item in a very strange place or in a place that you swear you checked already. One particular lost item success story comes to mind which was particularly amazing. A friend asked me about her lost wedding ring. I did not get the feeling it was really lost and I asked Archangel Chamuel for help in locating my friend's ring (since Chamuel is the lost item specialist). She mentally asked as well. What is particularly amazing is that the ring had been missing for a year. Two weeks after we asked for help, she got a call from the man who had purchased their previous home. He asked if she had lost anything and she immediately responded that she wasn't sure she had lost it there but that her wedding ring was missing. He asked her to describe it and sure enough it was hers. He had found it wrapped up in some paper under one of the bathroom sinks.

Finding Lost Items

Chris, a client of mine, told me this story about asking the "find it" specialty angels to help locate his birth certificate:

I desperately needed to find my birth certificate which I hadn't seen in years in order to renew my driver's license. I have a room downstairs that ends up holding all of my "junk". I have many boxes of papers and documents in there and didn't even know where to start. Just a few minutes in, I was thumbing through a stack of notebook sized papers and noticed a small stack of photographs in the middle of the pile. I wouldn't have stopped to look at them except for the fact that they were of my Chesapeake Bay Retriever who I recently had to put down due to age. She was very special to me and I picked up the photos to look at them. When I went to set them aside I noticed a 5 x 5 inch piece of paper that had been lying underneath them face down. It was white but a little yellowed and was on top of a sheet of white paper. I instantly knew from its size what it was...I flipped it over and sure enough, my birth certificate from 1961! My girlfriend who has been to your Angel Seminar had told me earlier in the day to ask the Find It Angel for help, which I did. I am convinced this is the exact reason I was able to find this document!!!

Safety

Asking the angels to keep you safe is highly recommended, in general, but particularly if you are going to be doing anything that could be dangerous or where you might be vulnerable. A friend once told me an incredible story about a friend who asked the angels to protect her as she walked home one evening. The next day, she learned that another woman in the neighborhood had been murdered. She went to the police as she had walked home at approximately the same time to when the woman had been killed. They arrested the man and they asked why he hadn't attacked the other woman. He responded that she had two big men walking with her, so he had left her alone. The angels do have the ability to shift perception so there are many ways in which they can ensure you are safe.

Finding Love

The angels are fantastic counselors and relationship helpers. When you ask for help, pay attention to any signs you get and be open to their answers. Sometimes they may guide you to release an unhealthy relationship or they may give you tools to help you heal the relationship. You are not benefiting yourself or the other person by staying in an unhealthy relationship and the angels will only guide you in a healthy direction. You can also ask the angels to help you find your life partner or even Mister or Miss Right Now. Ask for help with what you want very clearly or you might get something that is not exactly what you are looking for. Keep in mind that sometimes we think we know what we want only to receive it and find out we don't.

That is ok, simply thank the angels for their assistance and let them know you have changed your mind and then ask for help with your new request.

I heard this great story from my friend Michael about his relationship prayer being answered very quickly!

One Sunday at church, we had a guest speaker named Sunny Dawn Johnson. She spoke of angels and how they are always there with us ready and able to help us with any and all desires. As in the past when I was impressed with a guest speaker, I purchased her book. But like many before her, I put the book away and never opened it again. Fast forward many months later, a dear friend from church who also spoke of angels gave a little talk in conjunction with a special service being held at the church. I respected this friend very much, and trusted her. I thought about what she said and realized I'd heard it once with Sunny Dawn Johnson, and now through my friend Laura. I decided I had better listen. I knew in the back of my mind that I had struggled with my weight. I thought unless I lost weight I would never meet the right guy. I hit rock bottom one night. I was lonely, I was praying, and I decided to call on my angels. I spoke like they were a good friend. I said, I KNOW the truth about me, is that I am whole perfect and complete despite what my ego or my own self-defeating thoughts think. I knew in my heart the truth about me was bigger. I asked my angels to bring into my life someone who loves me for me; someone who loves me exactly as I was right then and there, and that I would see myself through their eyes. Within a week, I met someone who I thought was just going to be a friend. He stated prior to us meeting in person, that he was not looking to date, he was just looking for a good friend. We had a wonderful dinner and evening the first night we met. It is safe to say it was love at first sight. We have been together now for almost 7 months. When I see myself as he sees me, I love myself a bit more every day. I do believe my angels helped bring us together. I think it is as easy as asking but many of us do not ask in earnest. Partly because we don't believe it's that easy. It is easy as 1, 2, 3, and our Angels are just thrilled to help us.

Our thoughts are like instant prayers to the universe. We have all heard of the law of attraction and it truly does work. We don't want what we worry about to happen, but worry and fear are like prayers sent out to the universe. The problem is the universe delivers to us what we think about whether it is what we want or not! We are taught to worry but the truth is that this is the worst thing we can do! If you catch yourself worrying, don't berate yourself. Just notice what you are doing, change your thought and ask the angels to help you stay positive and filled with faith.

It is important to have faith that our requests for guidance and assistance have been answered. If we don't believe or have faith, this can slow down or block our guides' ability to help us. If we ask for help but don't believe that it is possible, our thoughts will literally keep the answer to our prayers at bay. This can seem like a "Catch 22", but since you can ask the angels and guides to help elevate your thoughts, all you have to do is ask them to help you with your faith and believe in miracles and the angels or guides will help you.

One excellent book that is about how we get in our own way is called *Outwitting the Devil*, By Napoleon Hill. Hill also wrote the famous book *Think and Grow Rich*. This is an incredible book that written in 1938 that was only released in 2011 because Hill's wife and family reportedly believed that the information included was so ground-breaking and controversial that others would not be able to accept it. I highly recommend this book for those who want to better understand how to have faith and release fear.

Housing Help

This next story shares how with faith, unlikely things do happen! A client of mine named Mary

O'Connor came to me for a reading who was in a great deal of transition. Her employment situation was ending which also happened to be where she lived since the managed the housing complex in which she lived. Not only was she going to be out of work, but she was looking for a place to live and she had three older cats. She was very concerned about her prospects and in particular about whether she was going to be able to find a situation that would allow her to keep her pets. The instruction from the angels was to create a list of the qualities that she wanted in a home and then to ask the angels for help. Mary did this, and as her deadline for moving out loomed, she became more and more concerned that she was going to have to give up her cats for adoption. None of the apartments that she looked at allowed one cat, not to mention three. One day before she planned to take her cats to a shelter, she found just the perfect place! It was in her budget in a beautiful location with a lot of land and the landlord was thrilled to have her and all her cats too. The angels answered her prayer just in time. This story illustrates the importance of keeping the faith even if it seems unlikely. If she had given up the day before, she would have taken the cats to the shelter and would not have found the place she was looking for.

Remember that no problem is too big or too small. You can pray for a hug, a piece of chocolate, or the man/woman of your dreams! Also know that you are not bothering the angels and guides when you ask for help, they want to help you! In fact, many times they want to help us and they sit idly by while we struggle on our own.

NINE

How to Help The Angels Answer Your Prayers

While angels can help us create incredible changes in our lives, there are many things that we can do to help them help us. Many of our day-to-day activities, thought processes and beliefs can actually block their efforts. Most of the time, we are not doing these things on purpose, so I'd like to share ways in which we can help them answer our prayers or help the changes happen more quickly. Most of these suggestions will likely help you feel better as well. I've listed several tips below and will go into more detail on why each of these is important.

How can you help angels answer your prayers?

- Faith
- Pay attention for signs
- Listen to your intuition
- Release fear and worry
- Keep asking for signs and guidance
- Feel gratitude
- Be positive
- Be open to alternative solutions as answers to your prayers

It is best to ask for help and listen to guidance constantly. Unfortunately, it does not work to say, "Help me with this from now on." Because of free will and our ability to change our mind, we must constantly ask for specific assistance. You must ask over and over again daily or sometimes several times a day for the help and guidance you want. For example, if you are asking for help releasing worry, you may have to do it several times a day.

Faith

Faith is a very important ingredient in the recipe for an answered prayer because if we do not have faith that our prayer is being answered, it can keep away our desired results. What we believe can happen absolutely impacts the outcome. If we ask for help, but on a deep level do not believe it is possible, that belief can keep the answer to our prayer away. But do not despair because we can ask the angels for help shifting our beliefs as well. Our word and thoughts are very powerful so it is important to monitor them. If we are thinking and saying things that are opposite of our prayer, this can prevent it from happening or slow down the manifestation.

Pay Attention to the Signs

I know I have mentioned this before but I think it bears repeating. One key step to helping our angels answer our prayers is to pay attention to signs we receive. The angels are constantly sending us signs and messages which are often in response to our prayers. These messages may not seem like the answer to our prayers; however there is always a connection somehow. For example, you might ask for help with finances and you keep getting messages about a particular person, city, or book, and it may be that the message has a direct connection to your request for help! Maybe that person has a job opportunity for you or the book will help you understand where your passion, purpose, and abundance are. If something comes up repeatedly for you in your life, just know that is not a coincidence. If you are not sure what you are sensing is a message from them, ask for a very clear sign and you will receive one.

This is very important because many times, the angels give us suggestions that will help us answer our own prayers through our actions. The divine often works through angels and other people to help us answer our own prayers as the following illustrates. This story has been told in various forms many times and this version is from the Epistle website:

> *A terrible storm came into a town and local officials sent out an emergency warning that the riverbanks would soon overflow and flood the nearby homes. They ordered everyone in the town to evacuate immediately.*
>
> *A faithful Christian man heard the warning and decided to stay, saying to himself, "I will trust God and if I am in danger, then God will send a divine miracle to save me."*
>
> *The neighbors came by his house and said to him, "We're leaving and there is room for you in our car,*

please come with us!" But the man declined. "I have faith that God will save me."

As the man stood on his porch watching the water rise up the steps, a man in a canoe paddled by and called to him, "Hurry and come into my canoe, the waters are rising quickly!" But the man again said, "No thanks, God will save me."

The floodwaters rose higher pouring water into his living room and the man had to retreat to the second floor. A police motorboat came by and saw him at the window. "We will come up and rescue you!" they shouted. But the man refused, waving them off saying, "Use your time to save someone else! I have faith that God will save me!"

The flood waters rose higher and higher and the man had to climb up to his rooftop.

A helicopter spotted him and dropped a rope ladder. A rescue officer came down the ladder and pleaded with the man, "Grab my hand and I will pull you up!" But the man STILL refused, folding his arms tightly to his body. "No thank you! God will save me!"

Shortly after, the house broke up and the floodwaters swept the man away and he drowned.

When in Heaven, the man stood before God and asked, "I put all of my faith in You. Why didn't You come and save me?"

And God said, "Son, I sent you a warning. I sent you a car. I sent you a canoe. I sent you a motorboat. I sent you a helicopter. What more were you looking for?"

This story shows how our angels are tools of the creator, (in fact so are you!). God, or the creator, is always communicating through us, often through angels, animals and other people to assist us all. We are not used to thinking in these terms so we often miss the messages and the assistance that we are being sent. It is my hope that this book helps people recognize the messages and the assistance that we are offered on a regular basis.

Stress and Worry

One thing I am constantly being shown in readings when clients are asking for guidance about finances, romance, or career is the importance of being positive and releasing fear and worry. This is important for many reasons. One of the main reasons is that our thoughts act like instant requests to the universe. *The Law of Attraction* truly works. One piece of information that is not commonly known is that it is not just our thoughts that attract experiences to us but our emotions as well. So in essence, feeling worried will bring more worry to you. Feeling joy will bring you more joy, etc. While this might sound unfair, it is just how the system is designed. I believe it is this principle that the bible passage found in Matthew 25:29 is explaining. Here is the language pulled from the New International Version of the Bible:

> *For everyone who has will be given more, and he will have an abundance. Whoever does not have, even what he has will be taken from him.*

I believe this Bible passage has been largely misunderstood. I do not believe it means that if you have nothing, even that will be taken away and that if you have, you will be given more. I *do* however believe that if you *feel* you have nothing, what little you have will get taken away. What is important is not what you actually have but your feelings at the time. There are people in poverty who are positive and have lived through incredible trials and tribulations and come out of it all with incredible stories and a happy ending. Tererai Trent who was featured on the Oprah show is a wonderful example. She was born in Zimbabwe and was born poor, married young and had three children by the age of 18. Against all odds, she came to the United States, received her doctorate, and has been incredibly successful and is now raising money for a school in her home town. You can read more about her in the book *Half of the Sky*.

I have done readings for clients who were born into middle class families and who for all intents and purposes were born into a life of privilege, access and abundance but will say things like, "life has always been hard for me." And I am sure that is how they feel! I am not discounting that feeling, for we all have had times when life seemed a struggle. I do, however, want to point out that this type of feeling is not likely to bring you what you desire and makes it very difficult for our angels to help answer our prayers.

If you are struggling with feeling down, there is good news. Sometimes having perspective about what we do have can help a lot. If you are born in the United States you are likely lucky simply through statistics. According to *The Water Project*, one in eight people in the world still don't have access to safe drinking water which has a huge impact on one's wellbeing and lifestyle. Those folks don't have the luxury of thinking about high heeled shoes, finances, or job stress – they are just trying to stay alive. Sometimes remembering facts like this can help us feel better about our current circumstances.

One other great pointer is that angels can help us shift our worry. Archangel Michael is great for this job but even asking your guardian angel can help too. Don't beat yourself up for feeling down or worrying but do turn it into a request for help right away and ask the angels to turn your worry into faith. Done often and repeatedly, this can make a huge difference in your experiences and bring more of what you want, and less of what you don't want.

Gratitude

Because the law of attraction works to bring you more of what you think about, and more importantly more of how you feel, living in gratitude is sure to help you. You can feel grateful about the little things, the food you are eating, the people in your life, your health. Be grateful for whatever you have, even if initially you think you don't have much, and you will likely start to notice how many wonderful things and experiences life is presenting you. If you don't like what you experience, take note and then start to change your patterns and ask for help with what you do want. It is very important to focus on what qualities you want in your life rather than what you don't. Feeling grateful for what you don't already have is very likely to bring that very thing or experience to you because of how the law of attraction works. For more information on the law of attraction, you can read *The Law of Attraction Made Simple* by Jonathan Manske.

Keep Asking

As you go through this process and start changing your life for the better, be sure to keep asking for signs and guidance from your spirit guides and angels, that way you are sure to keep moving in the best direction for you. Be sure to follow the signs and do what feels right for you rather than what other people tell you. This is particularly true if you are around people who are skeptical about angels and the law of attraction. People will often try to shut down your new beliefs if they have a mindset which does not support the possibilities that this mindset allows. There is no reason to be angry or frustrated or to look down on others as every person's path is different. Sometimes the best way to teach others is to demonstrate what is possible.

Be Open to Alternatives

As you start on your path, be open to alternative answers to your prayers. This can mean that you receive whatever it is that you desire in a non-traditional way. For example, as I opened up to my gifts, I was newly unemployed and the way I had been taught to receive financial support was through a traditional job. I tried again and again to find a job but nothing worked out which was a new experience for me. I had always found employment easily. I've realized now that this is because that was not my path. The angels were sending me signs that my path to abundance was through working with angels and spirituality and not through a traditional *job.* It was so hard for me to believe that I resisted the guidance for some time. If I had paid attention, I am sure my finances would have improved much faster and I would have spent a lot less time applying for jobs that never came through. I want to stress that this is my story, and everyone's path is different which is why it is important to pay attention to the signs.

One last thought I'd like to share about this process is that your life can change very quickly and miraculously when you believe and listen to your guidance. Something might seem too good to be true but may only seem that way because you have been taught that your life must be hard. Pay attention to what you feel rather than what you think and ask for signs and clarification on your journey. Once you start living your life this way, life can seem magical for there are very few limits in life when you are following divine guidance. We are here to create our lives as we like, and how we do that is up to us; we can use our guidance to steer the ship to have a truly magical adventure.

TEN

Angel Miracle Stories

Throughout the last several years, I've had many experiences which were truly miraculous and I'd like to share a few of them here to give you real life examples of just some of the things that are possible. This is just a small sampling of modern-day miracles which have happened to me or people I know. Please know that miracles like these and more are possible for you if you ask for assistance and believe that they are possible. For the purposes of this book, I will use the Oxford English dictionary (2nd edition) definition of miracle, "A miracle is an event not ascribable to human power or the laws of nature and consequently attributed to a supernatural, especially divine, agency." There are many types of miracles, large and small; here are a few that I have experienced and witnessed.

Mechanical Miracle

One Saint Patrick's Day, I was heading down to Denver with a friend to watch the parade. We exited the highway and hit terrible traffic due to the parade route. This was not unexpected, but the traffic was worse than I had anticipated and we found ourselves sitting in traffic and barely moving for an hour. It was quite hot and very sunny that morning and as we sat the engine started to overheat. We watched as the temperature gauge rose and before long the engine was emitting steam in front of us. In fact, people were honking and pointing at the engine of the car to make sure we knew. Our steaming engine was getting us a lot of attention because it was so dramatic looking.

There was nowhere to go because we were stuck in traffic so I called on the resources I had – the angels! I asked Michael (a wonderful handyman), Raphael (for help with transportation) and all the mechanical and fix-it angels to help us and fix the engine. I did this for several minutes and focused very intently on my request. As I opened my eyes, the engine was starting to steam less. It stopped steaming and the temperature gauge went down and the engine cooled even though we continued to crawl along in traffic for at least 20 more minutes. The temperature outside remained high and by logic alone, the engine should have continued to overheat. I thanked the angels profusely for all their help and I knew that I had just witnessed a miracle.

Miracle After a Mugging

A friend of mine told me an incredible story about events that happened after he was mugged. My friend lived in the Capitol Hill neighborhood of Denver. One night he was walking home after a night out and was mugged by two men who hit him in the head with a tire iron before stealing his wallet. He was stunned, and bleeding badly from his head and sitting on the sidewalk trying to figure out what to do, when a woman pulled up in a car. She told him she was a nurse who'd just gotten off of work and offered to take him to the hospital. He got in her car and she drove him to the hospital. When they arrived, she helped him get inside and check in. After he was checked-in at the hospital, she said goodbye and left. During the process he noted how wonderful it was that she had been there to help and made a mental note to thank her later. The staff at the hospital gave him several stitches and checked him out.

The next day he took flowers to the hospital where she had told him she worked. When he arrived there with the flowers in hand, he was told that no-one by that name or that matched her description worked there. He was stunned and surprised but in looking back it made some sense. The woman had appeared late at night, just when he needed her, she gave a plausible story for him to believe her, and didn't seem to mind having a bleeding stranger in her car. After he was safe, she disappeared and was not seen again. Many other people tell similar stories of rescue or assistance in desperate situations. I believe that this also happens even when we don't ask for assistance if we are going to die before it is our time. This is one of the few instances in which an angel will intervene whether we ask for help or not.

Stories like this usually have several things in common. For one, the angel usually arrives just when needed and is a perfect fit for the job. They often have a van or vehicle for the job, they are friendly and help without asking for anything in return. They might even have a phone number on the van, or give you a business card, or a name which is a dead-end when researched. If something like this has happened to you, you very likely were helped by an angel!

Road Trip Miracle

Here is a story about an unexpected miracle on a road trip. I heard this story from Troy Mayer, who the angels connected me to on a recent trip to Las Vegas:

I was driving across the country on I - 70, leaving Vegas to Philly. Going through Utah and running low on gas but thought could make it to the next exit and gas station. That is when it got crazy. There were no more signs, just nothing but the road ahead and I was freaking out. The gas light came on and was on for a long time and still there was no gas station in sight. I started panicking. I got the feeling that someone was in the passenger seat. I looked over and I felt like someone was in the car. Then the car started shaking and was running out of gas. I was a young black dude in the middle of Utah and it is 25 degrees outside and it was 85 when I left Vegas – not good weather or circumstances to be stranded in. I started rocking back and forth and praying. In the distance, I saw a rest stop with a gas station. I thought I was seeing things. The car shut off due to lack of gas and the steering wheel locked. I guided the car to the exit ramp and when I made it down the ramp was going 2 miles an hour and I was ecstatic to make it. There were no people inside at the gas station. There was only one truck there. This guy comes over and asked if I need help. He has a hunting vest on and a hunting hat on. He started talking to me and then pumping gas for me. He said he knew the person who owned the gas station so he gave me the gas for free. He had a beautiful brand new GMC truck and says he lived "over yonder," and pointed in the distance. I got the tank of gas and go on my way. I am waving to the guy in my rearview mirror and he is waving at me and there is dirt kicking up behind me on the road. I glance back in the rearview mirror and when the dust settles, the man is gone, and so is the gas station. Later, I look up on the map and can't find this gas station or the rest stop. Earlier I felt like someone was in the car and now I am sure there was someone there helping me.

This story is a perfect example of angels intervening when things get really tough! The gas station materialized at just the right moment, the man helped Troy and was very friendly and after the help was received – there were no signs that he had been there and no way to find him again. These kinds of miracles happen in emergency situations after we ask for help and when there aren't people around that the angels can send to us.

Medical Miracle

The angels can also help you heal completely or help you get through an illness in a shorter duration of time or with less discomfort. When you ask for healing help, make sure to pay attention to any signs they might send you or ideas you get. Keep asking over and over again and affirm your health.

A relative of another client relayed this story to me after he was advised by my client to ask for help with healing:

I was having a particularly hard night. I was panic stricken, desperate and having a lot of pain all over my body. I wasn't sure if I was awake or asleep. I remembered what my daughter told me the day before about asking for help from spiritual helpers. I cried out "I need help!" Instantly I became aware of beings beside me, on both sides. I don't know how I knew, but I knew that the person on the left was the main one who was going to help me. I could see his arms. They were covered with petal or leaf shaped tattoos. The tattoos changed to where they were shaped like symbols or designs. And then they disappeared.

The person, whoever it was, became relaxed, not doing anything. I became relaxed when he did. I became peaceful and the panic disappeared. The other beings in the room nodded in agreement. There were three or four of them and all I could see of them was their eyes, blue and brown and black. One of them shook my hand and said, "thanks for letting us come."

The result of the visitation was peace. They didn't seem to do anything specific to me but afterwards I felt peaceful and didn't have any pain the whole day. I haven't had panic to that degree since then either. ~ Tom Barricklow

These stories are just a few examples that have happened to those I know and those in my circle. Miracles like this are happening every day!

ELEVEN

Final Thoughts

The stories and tips in this book are meant to help you connect with the angelic realm. There are many ways to do this and this book gives some examples. I encourage everyone to follow their intuition in this area as I am sure there are other ways to connect. The angels want to connect with you and are simply looking for an invitation. Often just a thought inviting their assistance is enough to experience great change and connecting with them regularly can help you have even greater life changes!

How angels fit into the big picture

Angels and spirit guides are here to help, assist, and guide us on our journey in this life and beyond. They are part of a much bigger, connected system that we belong to as well. The truth is that all of us are connected, we are all one and our angels and guides help us bridge a gap that we feel is there. The idea of separation is, in actuality, just an illusion. Part of the purpose for our life is to experience the illusion of separateness so that we can be the creators of our experience. Everything in this world is connected and that means that essentially we are one. Angels are a part of God and so are we. Jesus was the son of God but so are we; we are all a part of God's family.

The old phrase "as above, so below" applies here. That is one reason why it is a good idea to call on angels. We are the workers in the physical plane. In essence our angels and spirit guides are wanting and working on the same things on the energetic plane that we are working on in the physical plane. We are partners and we all want the best outcome. That is one of the biggest kept secrets of all! We're all in this together and the more we cooperate with our partners on earth and our divine helpers, the better it is for all of us.

The spiritual plane and the earth plane are like two halves of a whole. The material world and the spiritual world are connected, much like a tree's roots are just as much a part of the tree that I above ground portion. What happens above the ground absolutely affects the below ground world just as the below ground world affects the tree above and vice versa. You cannot separate the two. Heaven and the earth are intertwined just like this. The whole tree thrives only when both are doing well. Keep this in mind so that you never have a problem asking for help.

Afterward

As you go on this journey of recognizing your spirituality and connecting with your guides, you are likely to experience great shifts and changes in your life. This is a part of the process and is to be expected when you start working with angels. As these changes occur, do your best not to worry. Change can feel stressful but stress is only created by our reaction to what is happening. On a physical level, stress causes hormones to be released in the blood that are very damaging and lead to disease. In fact it is a great deal of disease is caused by stress. For more information on this, you might find it helpful to read the *Biology of Belief* by Bruce Lipton. On an energetic level this is also very important because we are creating our present experience and our future through our thoughts and feelings. In other words, we are manifesting what happens to us in the future based on what we think and how we feel. When we feel stress this brings more stress. As you start to shift, if you feel stressed, ask the angels to help you release that stress and feel comfort. Remember that not only is stress no fun but it also doesn't help – in fact it hinders! Keep talking with your angels and listening to their guidance; things will start to feel better.

I'd like to share imagery that came up in a reading regarding this journey we are all going through. A client who was very empathic and struggled with taking on other people's energy asked for information that would help. I was shown that we are all butterflies in the process of making the transformation. All of us are at different stages of this shift and all of us are making the change at different paces. One of the things that happens when a butterfly is transforming from a caterpillar to a butterfly is that it goes through this transformation in a chrysalis. In the chrysalis, all of the cells inside are rearranged and honestly, if you cut open the chrysalis it would look like a mess inside. Sometimes mess needs to be created in order to transform into the next phase of evolution. This is natural. Keep this in mind if your life is in upheaval and seems like it is falling apart. Sometimes in transition, all signs point to destruction and chaos when something new is actually being born. You can read more about this in the book *Spontaneous Evolution* by Dr. Bruce Lipton and Steve Bhaerman. Do not fear this change and keep asking for help from your angels to help the transition feel as smooth as possible.

Another helpful tip if this is new for you is to keep in mind that not everyone is open to working with angels and the spiritual world in this way. There are a lot of naysayers out there and they may be your best friend or your parent. Sometimes if we are excited and we tell our well-meaning loved ones about this, they rain on our parade! They usually are not doing this on purpose and often times, they mean well and want to spare us disappointment. Rather than tell people while you are new to this process, you might want to wait until you experience changes and then tell people about the success you've had through your work with angels and spirit guides. There are some people who will probably never be convinced and that is alright too, they are on their own path. Sometimes the best way to help others is to show them what is possible, not just for you but for them as well.

I want to express gratitude to you for reading this book and I know the angels are thankful too! There are many unemployed angels out there and the whole world will be a better place if we can all get them to start helping us. Because we are all connected, as you change your life, so changes the world. One person can truly make a difference.

I wish you the best on your path and adventure and I hope that you are as astonished and pleased with your experiences connecting to and receiving help from the magical angelic realm. Miracles happen every day and whether we experience them often has to do with whether we believe they are possible. I invite you to believe in the impossible, the magical, and in miracles. Believe in them and open the door to the miraculous in your own life.

Sending you love and light,

Laura Powers

Archangel Michael by Laura Smith Roccatani

Helpful Terms

Access Consciousness™: A system of removing old blocks and patterns using pressure applied to meridians that are believed to connect with specific patterns and beliefs.

Akashic Records – A record of an individual's lives as a soul. These are kept by Archangel Metatron.

Angel – a divine energy being. Angels are tasked with helping us with our life and life's work.

Angel Communicator – Someone who can communicate through one or more senses (sight, hearing, feeling) with angels.

Angelic Hierarchy (also called Celestial Hierarchy) – The hierarchy classifies the angels into specific ranks and orders which relate to the duties of that particular angel type. The most commonly referred to was created by Pseudo Dionysius, the Areopagite (member of a tribunal in Athens), a philosopher and Christian mystic.

Archangels – One of the orders of angels just above the angels in the Celestial Hierarchy. They have specialty areas and work more than the higher orders.

Ascended Master – A person who lived, experienced enlightenment and ascended so that they no longer need to incarnate for purposes of spiritual growth. Jesus and Buddha are two well-known ascended masters.

Celestial Hierarchy (also called Angelic Hierarchy) – The hierarchy classifies the angels into specific ranks and orders which relate to the duties of that particular angel type. The most commonly referred to was created by Pseudo Dionysius, the Areopagite (member of a tribunal in Athens), was a philosopher and Christian mystic.

Cherubim – The second highest order of angels in the hierarchy are described in the Old Testament many times. They are said to have guarded the Tree of Life in Eden with a flaming sword.

Clairalience – Clear-smelling or receiving information from your sense of smell; also called clairescence. This is a form of extra sensory perception or ESP.

Clairaudient – Clear-hearing or hearing sounds that are not just on the physical plane. This can be hearing a sound with your ears or hearing the word or phrase in your mind like a thought which isn't yours. This is a form of extra sensory perception or ESP.

Claircognizance – Clear knowing or knowing something you have no logical way of knowing. This is a form of extra sensory perception or ESP.

Clairgustance – The ability to taste something that you have not put in your mouth. This is a form of extra sensory perception or ESP.

Clairsentience – Clear feeling or feeling something that is coming from outside of you. This can be a physical sensation or emotion. This is a form of extra sensory perception or ESP.

Clairvoyance – Clear seeing or seeing something that is not on the physical plane. Clairvoyance can be experienced with your physical eyes or with your third or internal eye. This is a form of Extra Sensory Perception or ESP.

Cord – An energetic connection between people or people and places and things which transmit energies and emotions.

Dominations (also called Dominions) – The Dominations are said to rule over the lower orders and that they receive their guidance from the Seraphim and Cherubim.

Emotional Freedom Technique (EFT) ™ – A system that uses tapping to release old energy blocks, patterns and beliefs.

Empathy – The ability to feel what others are feeling. A form of Extra Sensory Perception or ESP.

Energy body – The energetic part of our body; we are made of matter and energy, and both parts come together to form our complete self.

Entity – An energetic being that does not have a physical form. Entities are non-human and they are not animals or angels either but some other type of being.

Extra Sensory Perception (ESP) – One or more heightened senses that perceives more than the normal range of sensing.

Ghosts – An earth bound spirit or the spirit of a person whose body has died and whose soul or spirit has not crossed into the light.

Kwan Yin – An eastern divinity being. Kwan Yin is believed to have been a real woman who became enlightened and instead of ascending into heaven, chose to help those on earth.

Medium – Someone who can sense and communicate with ghosts (earth bound spirits) and spirits (people without a body that are not earth bound) or other energy beings.

Miracle – An event that defies logical or practical explanation.

Parapsychology – A term coined in 1889 to describe research of the paranormal. Max Dessoir created the term by combining the words for “para” which means alongside, with the word psychology. The clair-senses, precognition, telepathy, psychokinesis, ghosts and other paranormal experiences are scientifically studied in parapsychology.

Powers – An order of angels, sometimes called the authorities. They are warrior angels and are said to act as an elite guard against dark forces.

Precognition – Knowing something is going to happen before it does with no logical way of knowing this. A form of Extra Sensory Perception or ESP.

Principalities – (Called Archai by some) They give blessings to the material world. They inspire people in the realms of art and science and are educators.

Psychokinesis – The ability to move matter with your mind.

Psychometry – The ability to receive information from an object through touch.

Sage – A plant that can be used to clear negative or stagnant energies. (Not the same as the herb sage).

Seraphim – The highest order of angels. The name Seraphim means the burning ones. The Ethiopian, Greek, and Hebrew words for Seraphim, translate as serpent, snake, or dragon. It is said that four Seraphim surround God and they burn from love.

Shaman – A person who is trained to communicate and work with the spirit realm. Shamans are found in indigenous cultures throughout the world.

Spirit – The non-physical manifestation of a person or being. The spirit never dies and is made of energy.

Spirit Guide – A being who is there to guide and support you. An advisor of sorts and they can take many forms from animals, to mythical creatures, angels, and loved ones who have crossed over.

Telepathy – The ability to communicate with others through thoughts.

Thrones – The third highest order of angels (also called the Ophanim by some) – The Thrones are described as being a wheel within a wheel and covered with eyes and emanating light.

Virtues – An order of angels who oversee the movement of the heavens.

Sources

These are books and websites that I reference for this book and that have informed me and my work.

ABC local. *Tragedy in Colorado*. 2012. http://abclocal.go.com/kabc/video?id=8744034

Access Consciousness. *Access Consciousness*. 2013. http://www.accessconsciousness.com/about-access.asp

Associated Press. *Aurora Police Chief says officers arrived at movie theater shooting within 60-90 second.* Star Tribune. 2012. http://www.startribune.com/nation/163213306.html?refer=y

Backman, Linda. *Bringing Your Soul to Light*. Llewellyn Worldwide Ltd., 2009.

Belanger, Michelle. *Psychic Vampire Codex: A Manual of Magick and Energy Work*. Red Wheel/Weiser, LLC, 2004.

Braden, Gregg. The Divine Matrix. Hay House Inc., 2007.

Bunick, Nick. *A Time for Truth*. Hay House Inc., 2010.

Biblos.com. Matthew 25:29. 2011.
http://bible.cc/matthew/25-29.htm

Byrne, Lorna. A Message of Hope from the Angels.
Coronet. 2012.

Byrne, Lorna. *Angels in My Hair*. Random House Digital,
Inc., 2009.

Calabrese, Adrian. *Sacred Signs: Hear, See and Believe
Messages from the Universe*. Llewellyn Publications,
2013.

Caldwell, Alicia. *James Holmes' Gun Jammed During
Aurora Attach, Official Says*. Huffington Post. 2012.
http://www.huffingtonpost.com/2012/07/22/james-holmes-gun-jammed-aurora-colorado-dark-knight-shooting_n_1692690.html

Chaudhary, Sufian. *The World of Archangels* .Sufian
Chaudhary. Sufian Chaudhary, 2013

Dionysius the Areopagite. *The Celestial Hierarchy*.n.d.

Einstein, A. *Albert Einstein Quotes*. Goodreads. 2013.
http://www.goodreads.com/quotes/101458-everybody-is-a-genius-but-if-you-judge-a-fish

Epistle. *God Will Save Me*. 2012. http://epistle.us/inspiration/godwillsaveme.html

Farmer, Steven. *Animal Spirit Guides: An Easy to Use Handbook for Identifying and Understanding Your Power Animals and Animal Spirit Helpers*. Hay House Inc., 2006.

Fast Company Staff. *Is $50,000 enough to buy Happiness? What about $161,810?* Fast Company. March 18, 2013. http://www.fastcompany.com/magazine/174/happiness-correlated-to-salary

Gregg, Susan. *Encyclopedia of Angels, Spirit Guides, and Ascended Masters: A Guide to 200 Celestial Beings.* Fair Winds Press, 2011.

Hill, Napoleon. *Outwitting the Devil.* Sterling Publishing. 2011.

Katz, Lynne. *You Are Psychic.* Llewellyn Worldwide Ltd., 2004.

Katrandjian, Olivia. *Colorado Movie Shooting: What a Miracle It Wasn't Worse*. ABC News. 2012 http://abcnews.go.com/US/aurora-shooting-miracle-worse/story?id=16829030#.UBWrw7QQuSo

Lipton, Bruce. *The Biology of Belief*. Hay House Inc., 2011.

McTaggart, Lynne. *The Field*. Harper Collins. 2009.

Merriam-Webster. Areopagus. 2013. http://www.merriam-webster.com/dictionary/areopagus

Michael, Todd. *The Hidden Parables: Activating the Secret of the Gospels.* Penguin Publishing, 2008.

Michael, Todd. *The Evolution Angel.* Penguin Publishing, 2008.

Murphey, Cecil and Piper, Don. *90 Minutes in Heaven: A True Story of Life and Death.* Revell, 2007.

Newton, Michael. *Journey of Souls: Case Studies of Life Between Lives*. Llewellyn Worldwide Ltd., 1996.

Nyland, A. Angels, Archangels, and Angel Categories: What the Ancients Said. Smith and Stirling. 2010.

Orloff, Judith, *M.D. Second Sight*. Warner Books, Inc., 1996.

Perry, Yvonne. *Whose Stuff is This? Finding Freedom from the Thoughts, Feelings, and Energy of Those Around You.* Write On! 2011.

Powers, Laura, *Life and the After-Life: Notes from a Medium and Angel Communicator*, Laura Powers Publishing, 2012.

Ruiz, Don Miguel. *The Four Agreements: A Practical Guide to Personal Freedom (A Toltec Wisdom Book).* Amber-Allen Publishing. 2011.

Schwartz, Robert. *Your Soul's Gift: The Healing Power of the Life You Planned Before You Were Born*. Whispering Winds Press. 2012.

Schwartz, Rob. *Your Soul's Plan*: *Discovering the Real Meaning of the Life You Planned Before You Were Born.* Frog Books, 2009.

Sullivan Walden, Kelly. *I Had the Strangest Dream: The Dreamers Dictionary for the 21st Century.* Hachett Book Group, 2009.

Taylor, Sharae. *Archangels List*. 2012. www.angelsbysharae.com/Archangelslist.html

The Denver Channel. *Angel In Clouds Above Theater Vigil?* Scripps TV Station Group. 2012. http://www.thedenverchannel.com/news/31296155/detail.html?taf=den

The Free Dictionary. *Muse*. 2012.
http://www.thefreedictionary.com/Muse

The New American Bible. Benzinger Inc., 1970.

The Water Project. *Water is Only the Beginning*. 2012.
http://thewaterproject.org/

Venefica, A. *The Spiritual Meaning of Numbers*.
http://www.whats-your-sign.com/spiritual-meaning-of-numbers.html

Virtue, Doreen. *Angel Medicine.* Hay House Inc., 2004.

Virtue, Doreen. *Angel Numbers 101: The Meaning of 111, 123, 444, and Other Number Sequences.* Hay House Inc., 2008.

Virtue, Doreen. *Archangels 101*. Hay House Inc., 2010.

Virtue, Doreen. *Archangels and Ascended Masters*. Hay House Inc., 2004.

Virtue, Doreen. *Fairies 101: An Introduction to Connecting, Working, and Healing with the Fairies.* Hay House Inc., 2007.

Virtue, Doreen. *Goddesses and Angels*. Hay House Inc., 2006.

Virtue, Doreen. *Realms of the Earth Angels*. Hay House Inc., 2007.

Virtue, Doreen. *The Healing Miracles of the Archangel Raphael.* Hay House Inc., 2010.

Virtue, Doreen. *The Lightworkers Way*. Hay House Inc., 1997

Virtue, Doreen. *The Miracles of Archangel Michael*. Hay House Inc., 2008.

Van Praagh, James. *Ghosts Among Us*. Harper Collins, 2008.

Wetzel, Lois. *Akashic Records: Case Studies of Past Lives*. Hot Pink Lotus Pod., 2011.

Wikipedia. *Angel (Sarah McLachlan Song).* 2013. http://en.wikipedia.org/wiki/Angel_(Sarah_McLachlan_song)

Wikipedia. *Book of Topit*. 2013. http://en.wikipedia.org/wiki/Book_of_Tobit

Wikipedia. *Book of Enoch*. 2013. http://en.wikipedia.org/wiki/Book_of_Enoch

Wikipedia. *Celestial Hierarchy*. 2012. http://www.paranormality.com/celestial_hierarchy.shtml

Wikipedia. *Emotional Freedom Technique*. 2013. http://en.wikipedia.org/wiki/Emotional_Freedom_Techniques

Wikipedia. *Forbidden City*. 2013. http://en.wikipedia.org/wiki/Forbidden_City

Wikipedia. *Gabriel*. 2012. http://en.wikipedia.org/wiki/Gabriel

Wikipedia. *Miracle*. 2013. http://en.wikipedia.org/wiki/Miracle

Wikipedia. *Parapsychology*. 2012. http://en.wikipedia.org/wiki/Parapsychology

Wikipedia. *Seraphim*. 2013. http://en.wikipedia.org/wiki/Christian_angelic_hierarchy#Seraphim

Resources and Recommended Reading List

Akashic Records: Case Studies of Past Lives by Lois Wetzel chronicles the Akashic readings of 30 clients.

Angel Numbers 101 by Doreen Virtue introduces the idea that angels communicate with us through numbers.

Angels in my Hair by Lorna Byrne shares the story of one Angel Communicator's journey coming to terms with her gift.

Animal Spirit Guides by Steven Farmer discusses animal spirit guides and related topics such as totem animals.

Ask Your Guides by Sonia Coquette gives great and practical information about how to communicate with your spirit guides.

Bringing Your Soul to Light by Dr. Linda Backman provides an exploration of the soul journey through the past and between life regressions.

Ghosts Among Us by Van Praagh is a great book that sheds light on the potentially spooky subject of ghosts in an informative and enlightening way.

I Had the Strangest Dream by Kelly Sullivan Walden is a dream analysis book that has a modern approach with listings that don't appear in some other dream analysis books.

Journey of Souls: Case Studies of Life Between Lives by Michael Newton takes a fascinating look at our lives between lives. Newton methodically regressed patients and noted descriptions and stories of the afterlife, revealing a surprisingly ordered system for those who are in spirit form.

Outwitting the Devil by Napolean Hill is a great book to help understand how we can get in our own way and how to keep that from happening.

Positive Energy: Ten Extraordinary Prescriptions for Transforming Fatigue, Stress, and Fear into Vibrance, Strength and Love by Dr. Judith Orloff gives practical tips for better managing your energy.

Psychic Vampire Codex: A Manual of Magick and Energy Work by Michelle A. Belanger. This book gives some great tools and tips for managing energy and energy healing work. Do not be scared by the word vampire in the title.

Sacred Signs: Hear, See and Believe Messages from the Universe by Adrian Calabrese gives simple and easy to follow guidelines on how to ask for and receive signs from your angels and spirit guides.

Second Sight by Judith Orloff, M.D. chronicles Dr. Orloff's personal journey as an intuitive and healer. She is a psychiatrist who initially turned away from her gift but gradually learned to embrace it.

The Four Agreements: A Practical Guide to Personal Freedom (A Toltec Wisdom Book) by Ruiz, Don Miguel gives four suggestions for living based on Toltec Wisdom.

The World of Archangel by Sufian Chaudhary shares detailed information about the Archangels and different dimensions.

A Time for Truth by Nick Bunick addresses and documents the presence of angels in the author's life but also discusses important changes within Christianity over time.

Whose Stuff is This? Finding Freedom from the Thoughts, Feelings, and Energy of Those Around You by Yvonne Perry describes one woman's journey as an empath. It is an excellent resource for those who are empathic or clairsentient.

You Are Psychic: The Art of Clairvoyant Reading and Healing by Debra Lynne Katz addresses many tools you yourself can learn to heal yourself and others.

Your Soul's Plan by Robert Schwartz explores the premise that we all create a life-plan before we are born.

Recommended Movies

Jesus in India: This Paul David documentary looks at Jesus' missing years between the ages of 12 and 30 and explores the possibility that he went to the East. Historical evidence is examined and experts all over the world are interviewed.

Something Unknown is Doing We Don't Know What: A documentary that examines various phenomena such as telekinesis, precognition, and energy healing.

Thrive: A fascinating film that looks at many seemingly unrelated structures and systems such as banking, the energy industry, and health care, and strives to get us to look at our role in the system differently.

What the Bleep do We Know?: Interviews with scientists and authors, animated bits, and a storyline involving a deaf photographer are used in this docudrama to illustrate the link between quantum mechanics, neurobiology, human consciousness and day-to-day reality.

Stay tuned for Laura's forthcoming book about Manifesting with the Angels!

For additional information, go to www.healingpowers.net. To receive updates about Laura's books, speaking engagements, events, TV show and more, submit your info on the subscribe page.

NOTES

NOTES

NOTES

About the Author – Laura Powers

Laura is a medium, angel communicator, ghost whisperer, actress, singer, and author of *Life and the After Life – Notes from a Medium and Angel Communicator*. She received her bachelor's degree in theatre and her master's degree in Political Science from the University of Colorado. When she is not writing or traveling, you may find her singing, dancing, or exploring the unknown. You can find more information about her acting, singing and fiction writing on her website www.laurapowers.net. You can find more information about her work in this field on the website www.healingpowers.net. Laura is currently working on her next book and a screenplay.

Made in the USA
Coppell, TX
10 August 2021

Angels: How to Recognize, Understand, and Receive Their Guidance

Laura Powers

Cover Photo by Penny O Photography

Library of Congress Data Available Upon Request

ISBN 978-0-9883026-4-8

First Printing, September 2013